THE BEST DOODLING BOOK EVER

Activinotes

DAILY JOURNALS, PLANNERS, NOTEBOOKS AND OTHER BLANK BOOKS

Copyright 2016

NAME

ADDRESS

CONTACT NUMBER

EMAIL ADDRESS

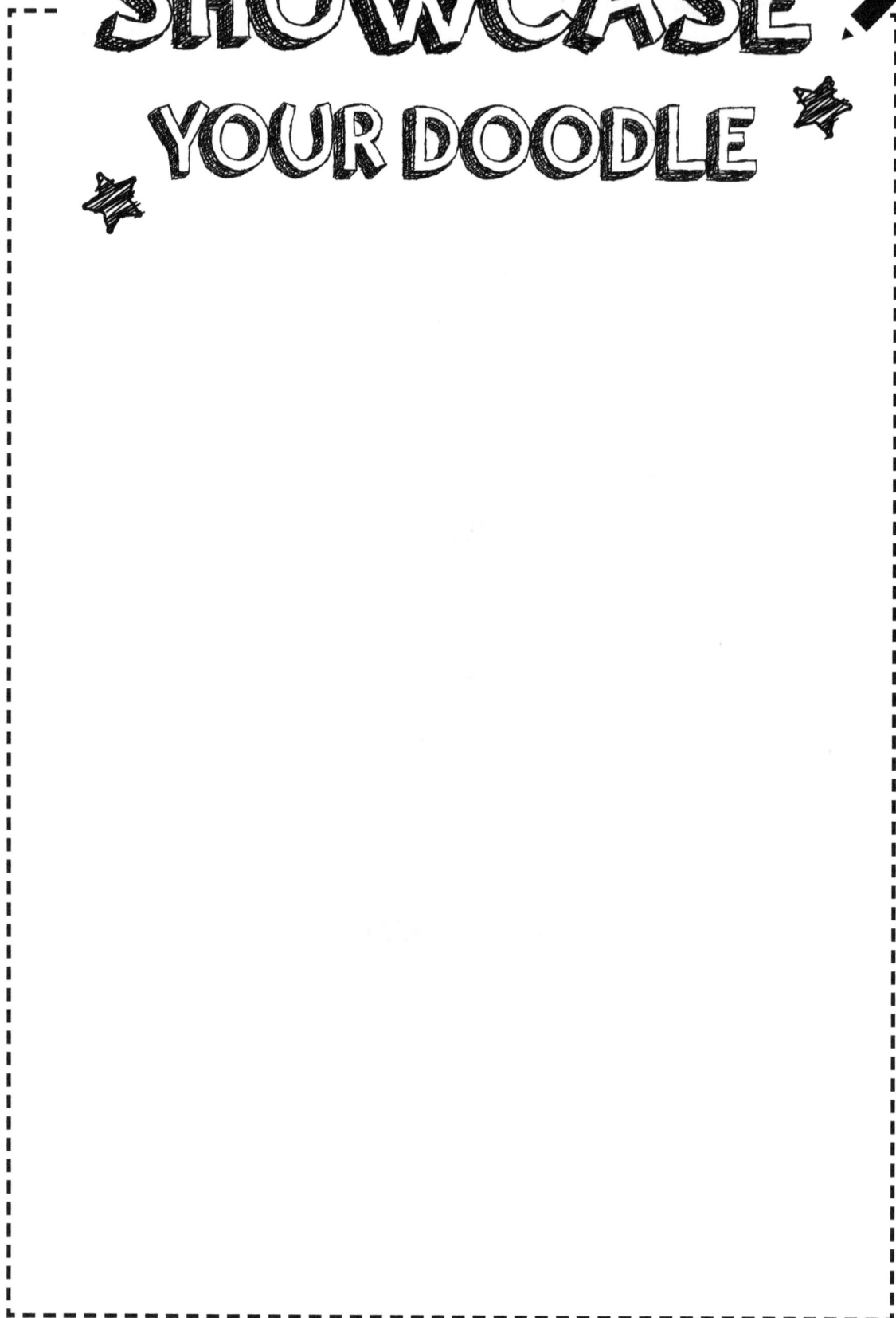

SHOWCASE
YOUR DOODLE

SKETCH

DRAW

CREATE

Doodle
and Beyond

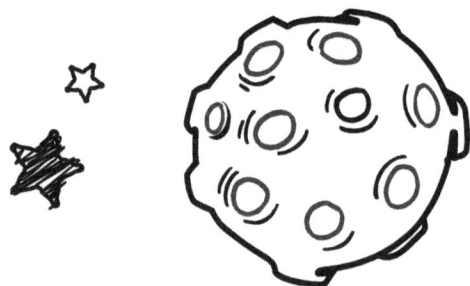

SHOWCASE
YOUR DOODLE

SKETCH

DRAW

CREATE

Doodle
and Beyond

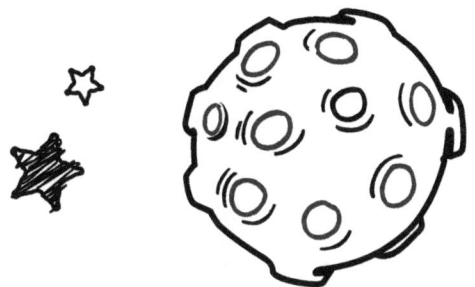

SHOWCASE
YOUR DOODLE

SKETCH

DRAW

CREATE

Doodle
and Beyond

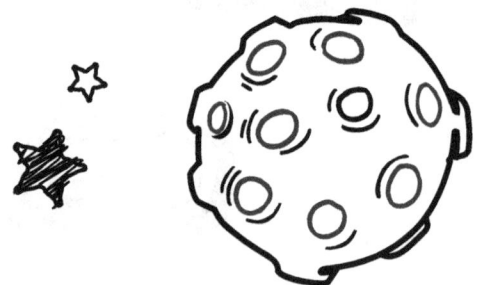

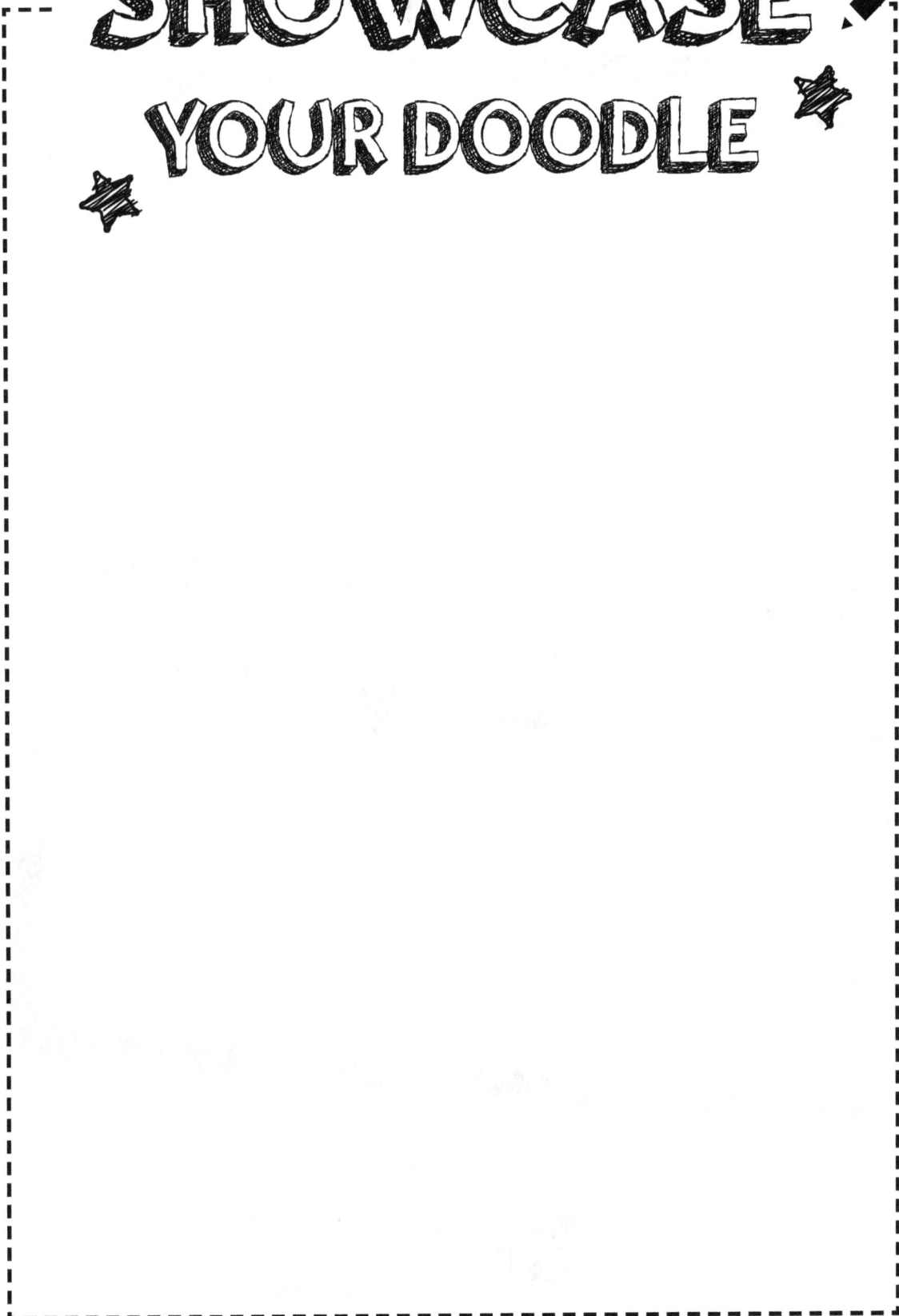

SHOWCASE
YOUR DOODLE

SKETCH

DRAW

CREATE

Doodle
and Beyond

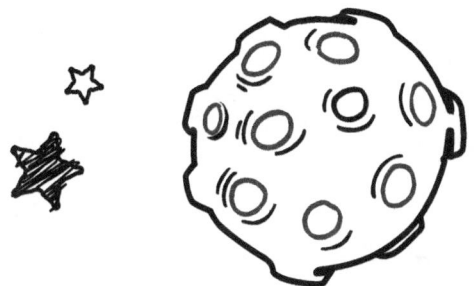

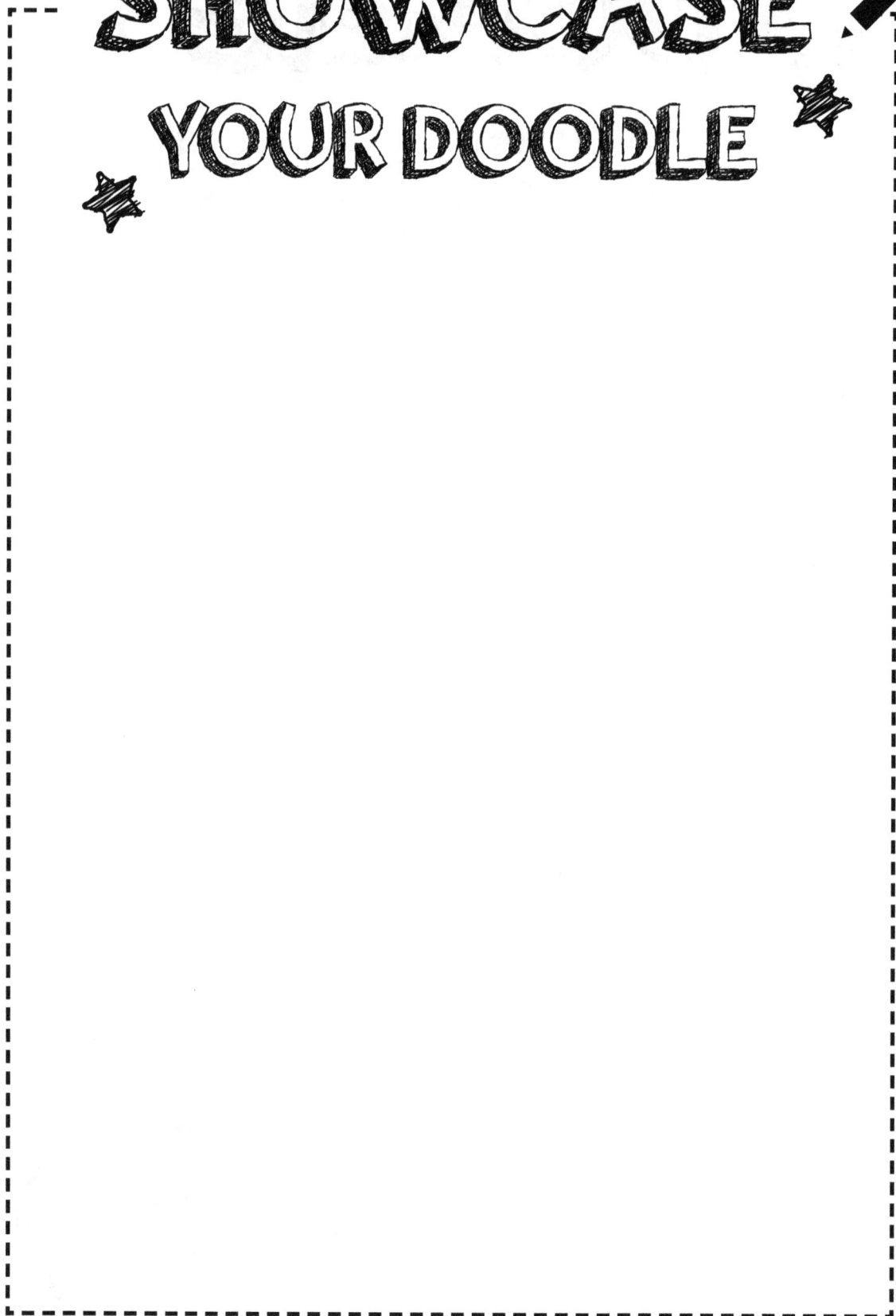

SHOWCASE
YOUR DOODLE

SKETCH

DRAW

CREATE

Doodle
and Beyond

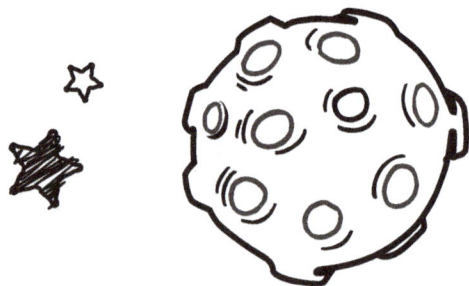

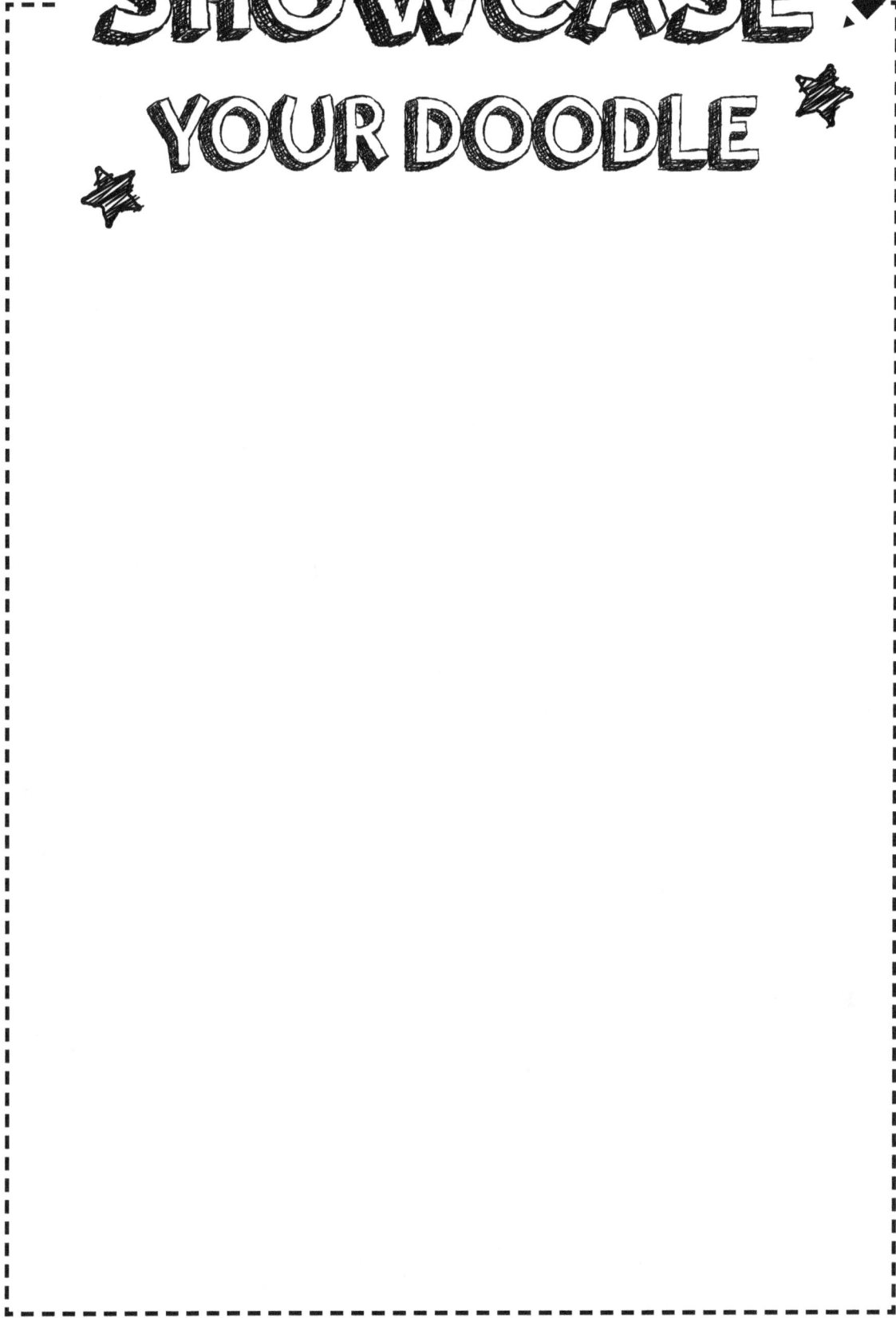

SHOWCASE
YOUR DOODLE

SKETCH

DRAW

CREATE

Doodle
and Beyond

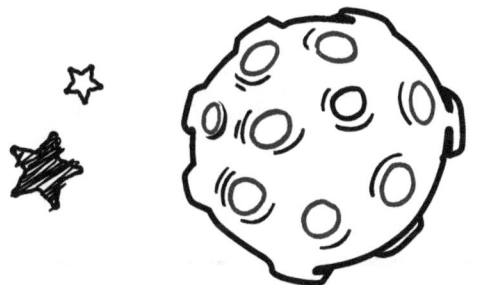

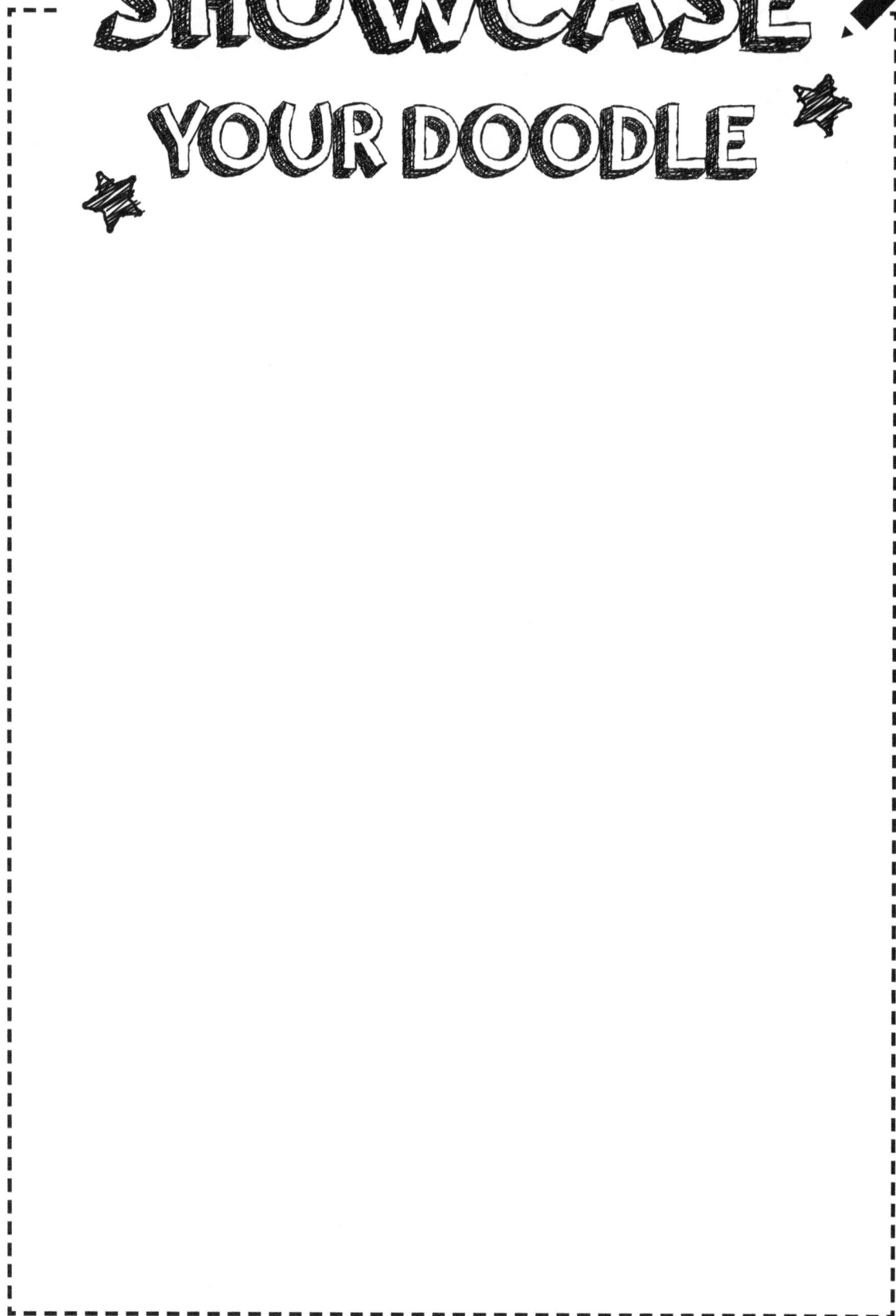

SHOWCASE
YOUR DOODLE

SKETCH

DRAW

CREATE

Doodle and Beyond

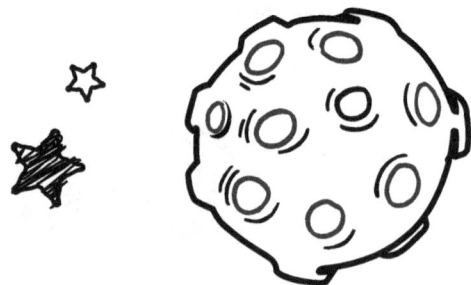

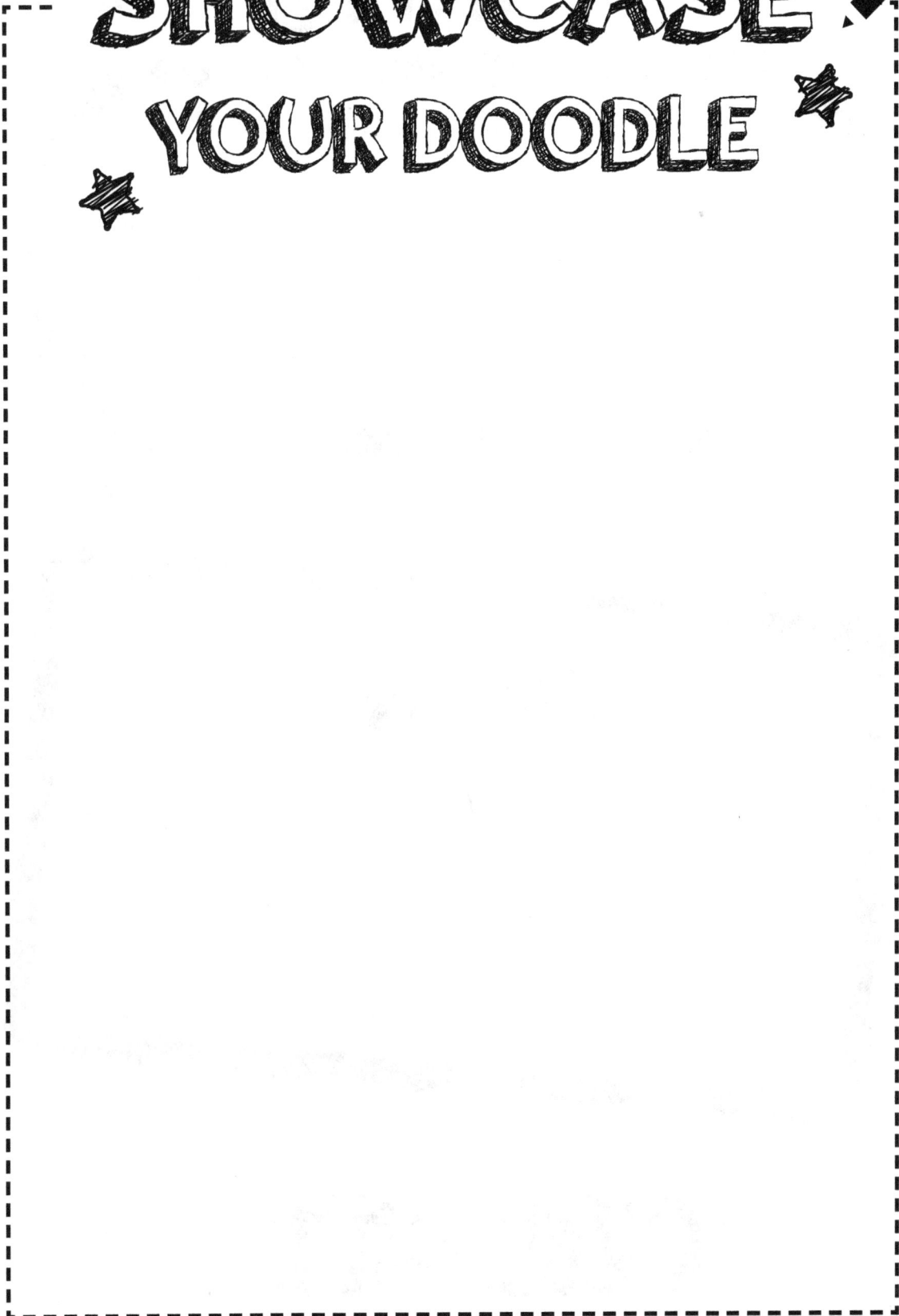

SHOWCASE
YOUR DOODLE

SKETCH

DRAW

CREATE

Doodle
and Beyond

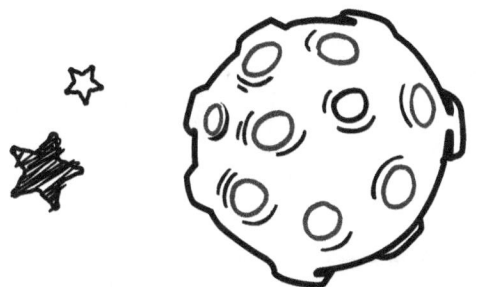

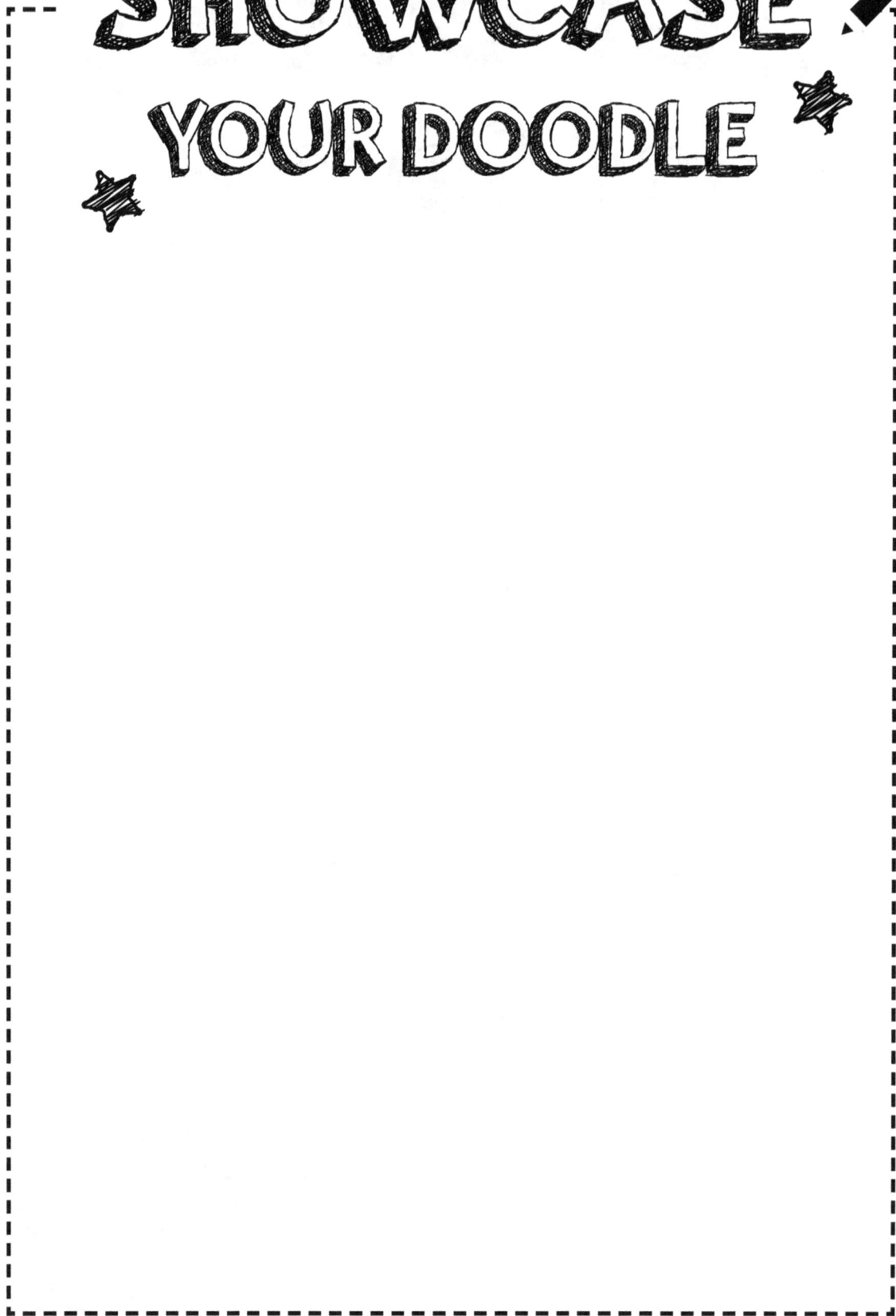

SHOWCASE
YOUR DOODLE

SKETCH

DRAW

CREATE

Doodle
and Beyond

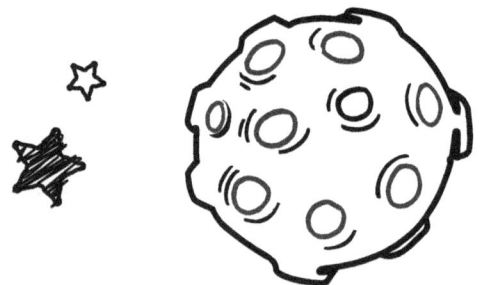

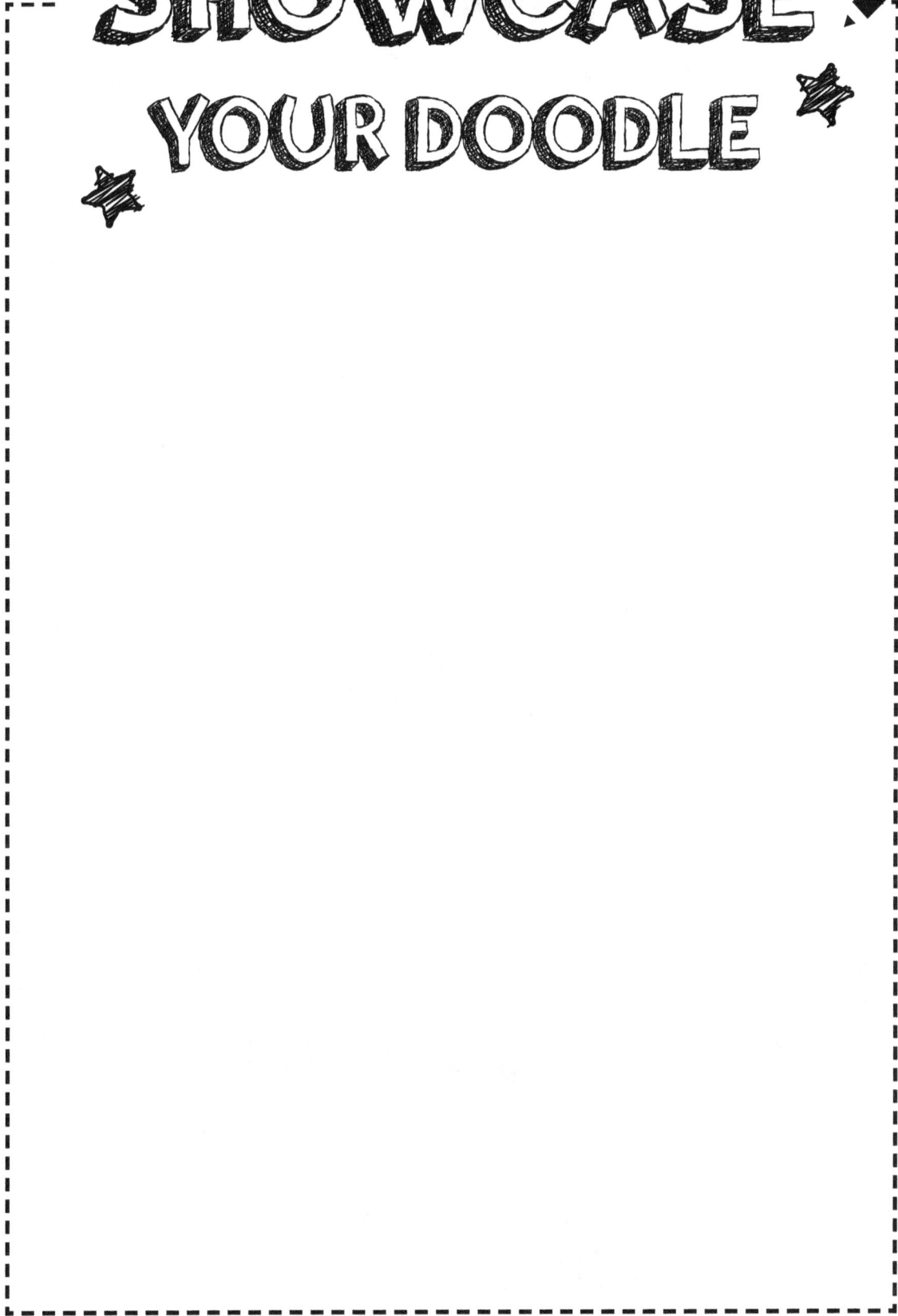

SHOWCASE
YOUR DOODLE

SKETCH

DRAW

CREATE

Doodle
and Beyond

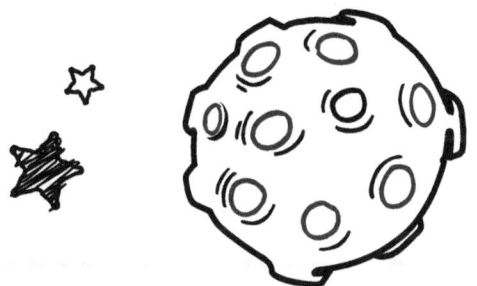

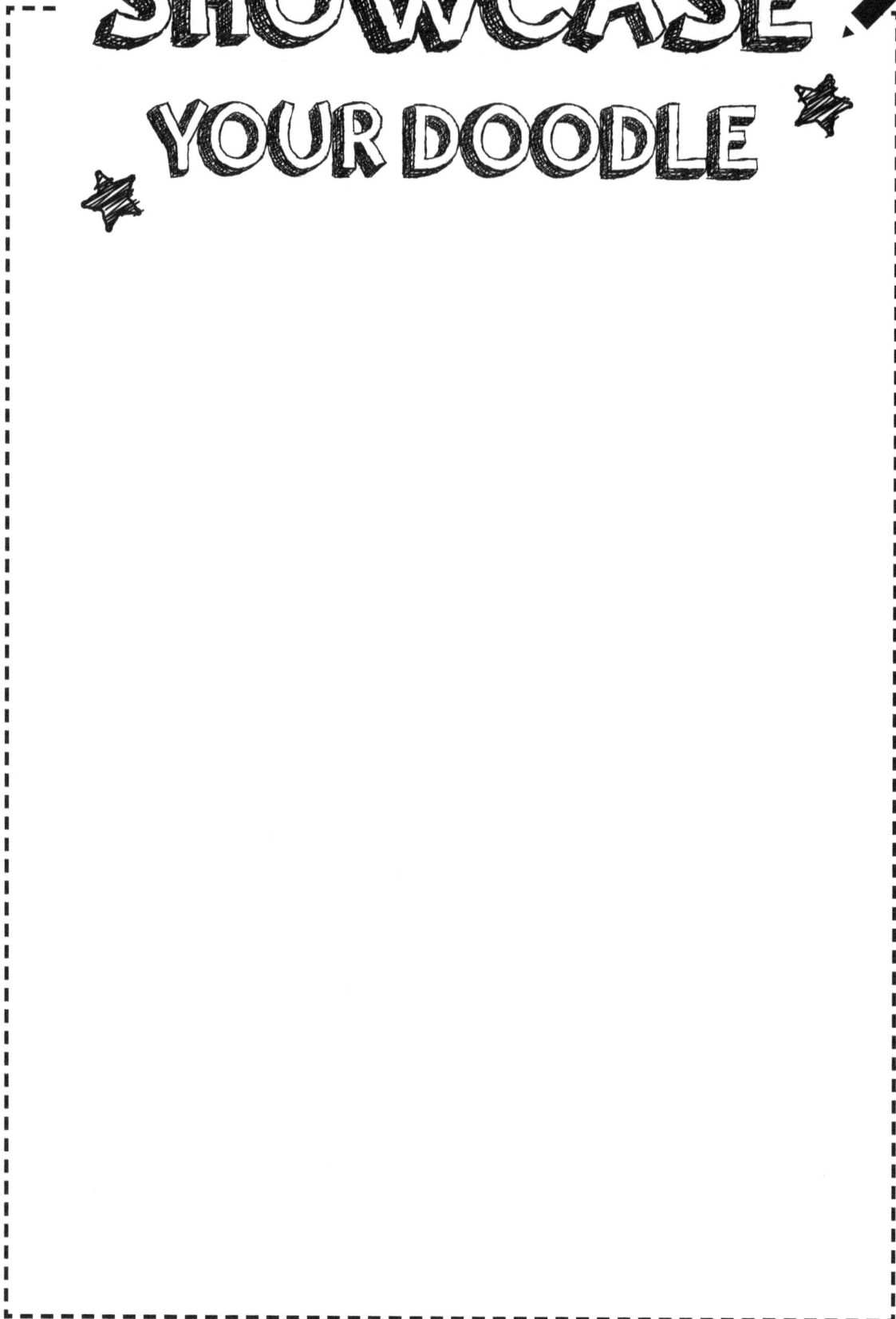

SHOWCASE
YOUR DOODLE

SKETCH

DRAW

CREATE

Doodle
and Beyond

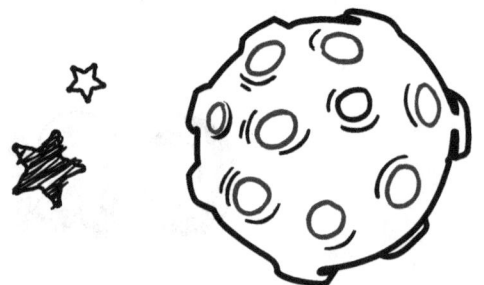

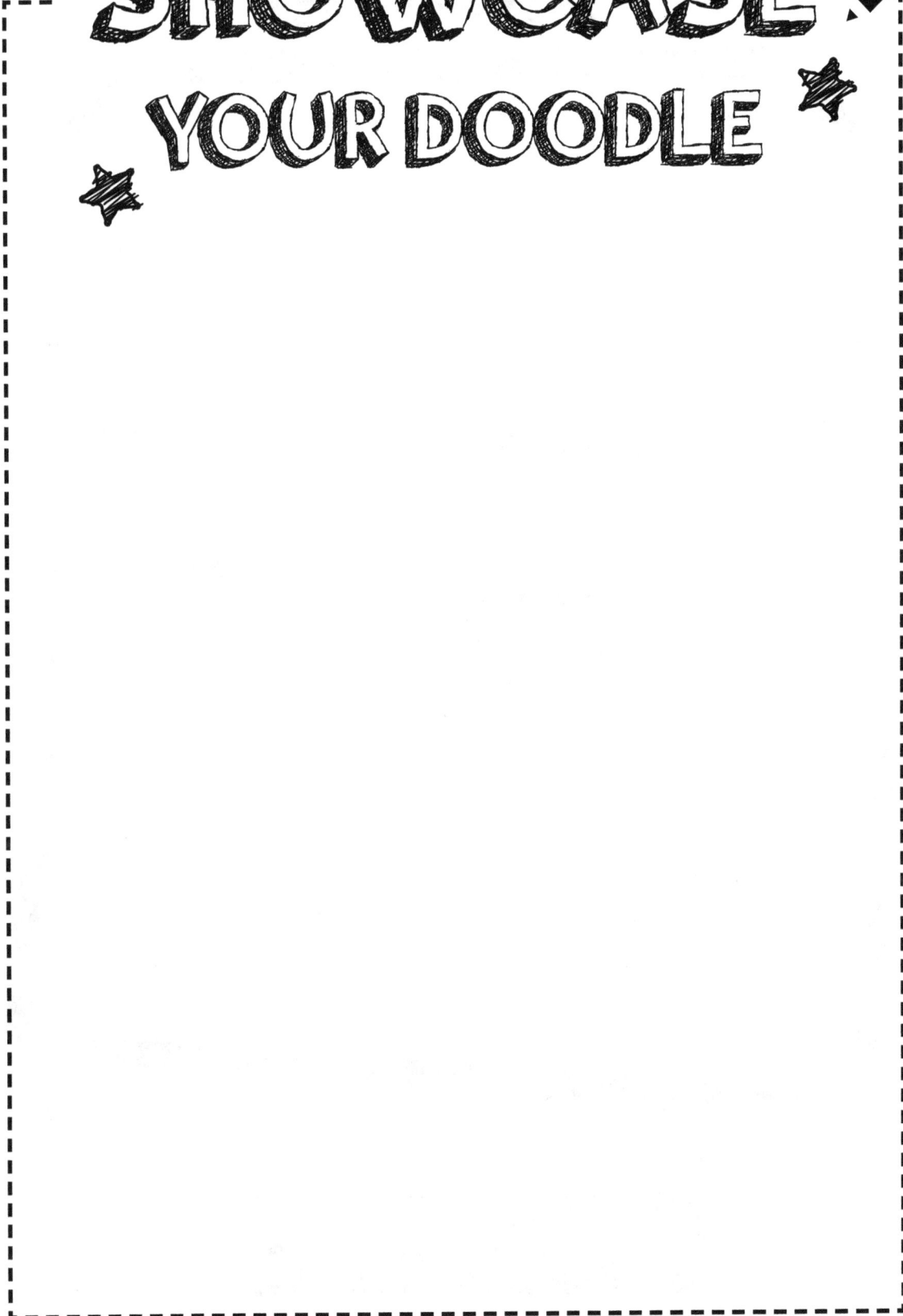

SHOWCASE
YOUR DOODLE

SKETCH

DRAW

CREATE

Doodle
and Beyond

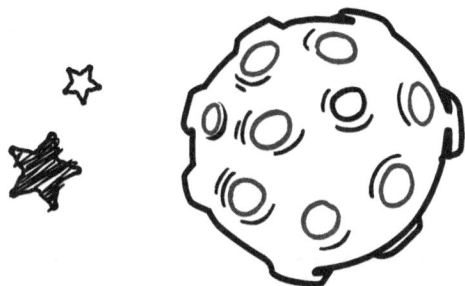

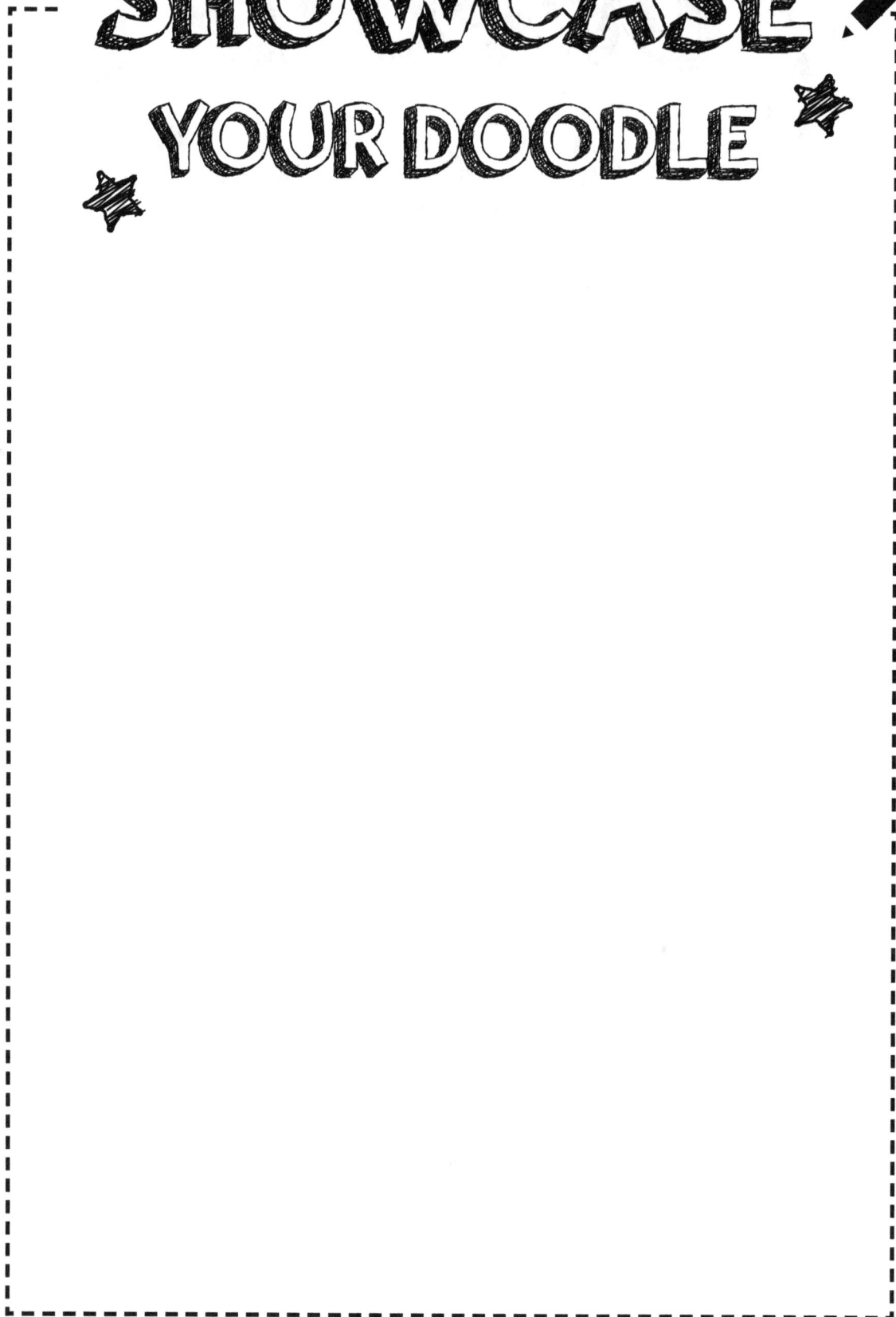

SHOWCASE
YOUR DOODLE

SKETCH

DRAW

CREATE

Doodle
and Beyond

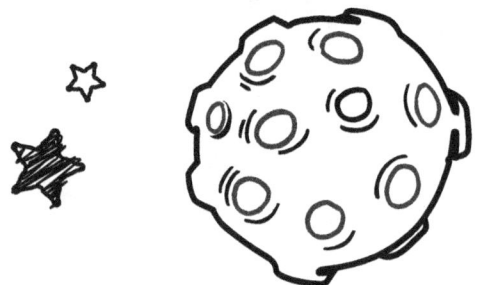

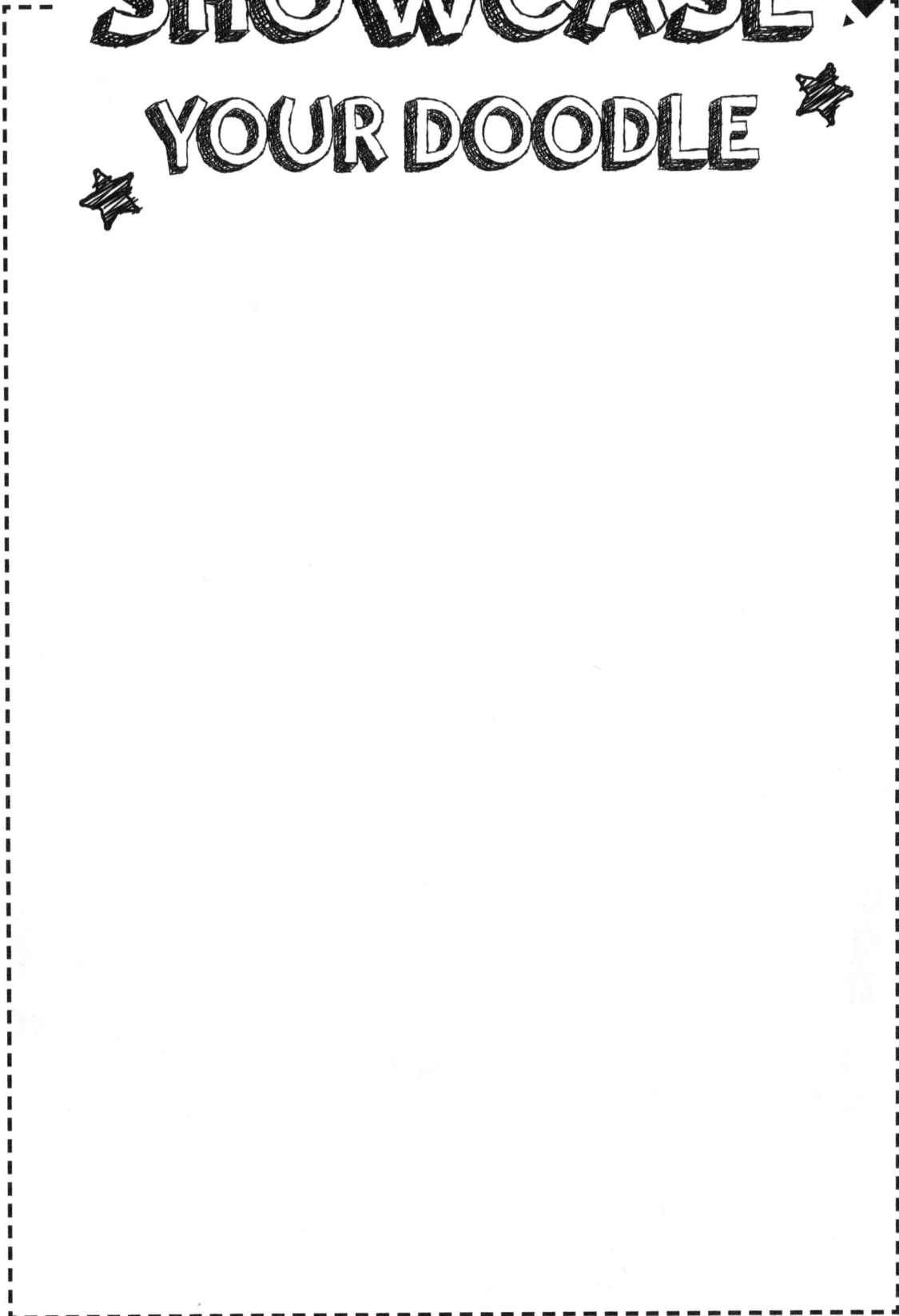

SHOWCASE
YOUR DOODLE

SKETCH

DRAW

CREATE

Doodle
and Beyond

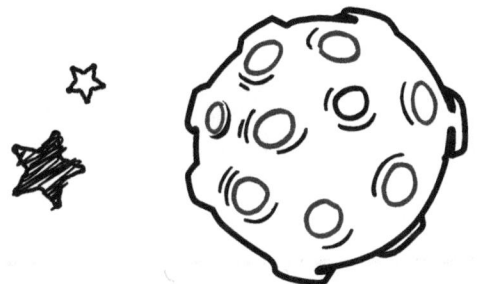

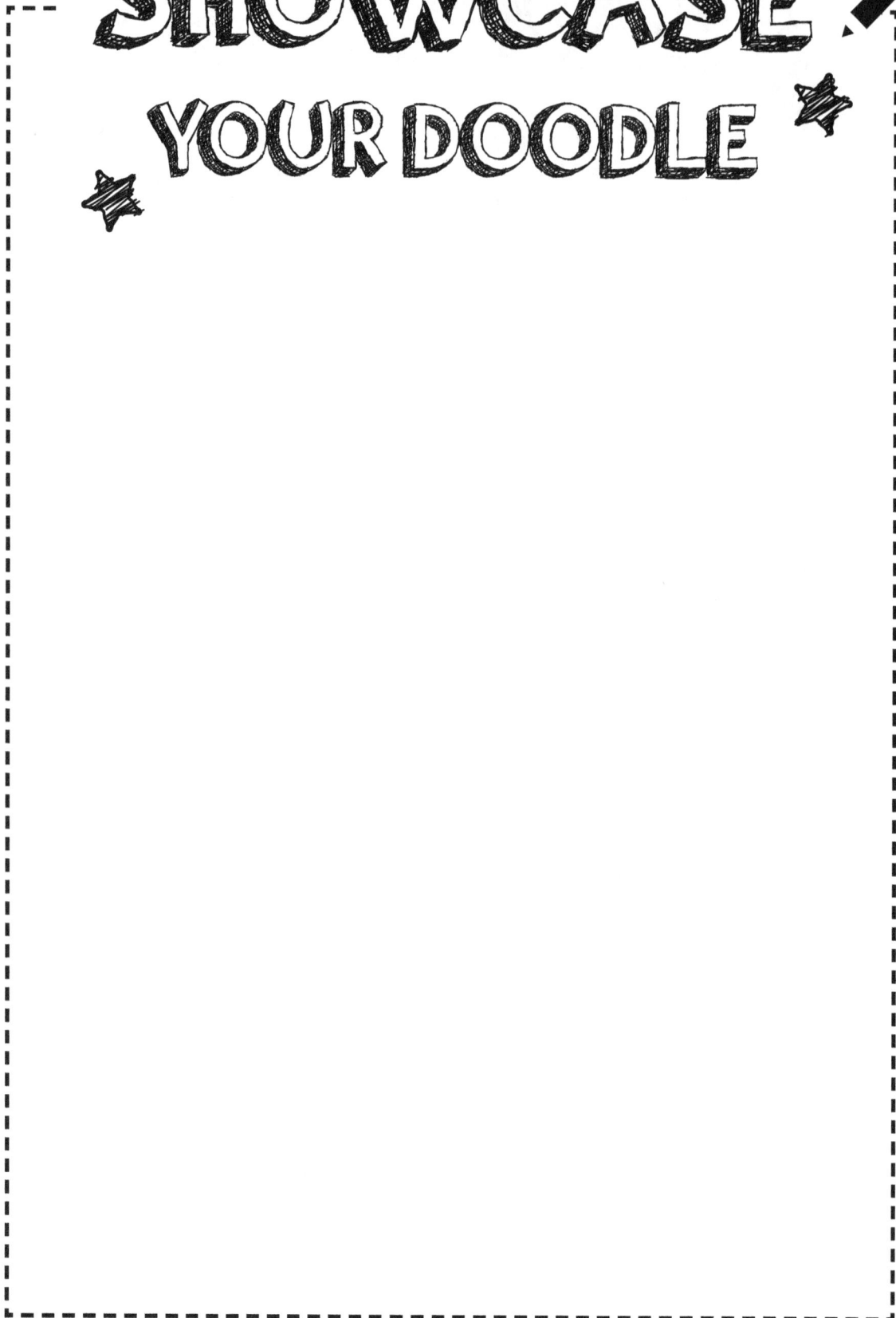

SHOWCASE
YOUR DOODLE

SKETCH

DRAW

CREATE

Doodle
and Beyond

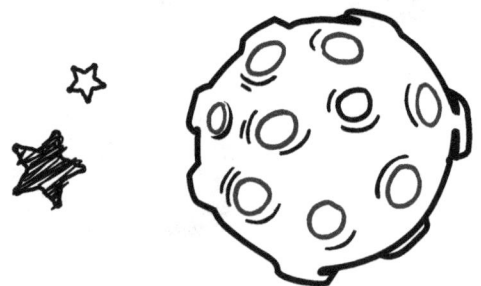

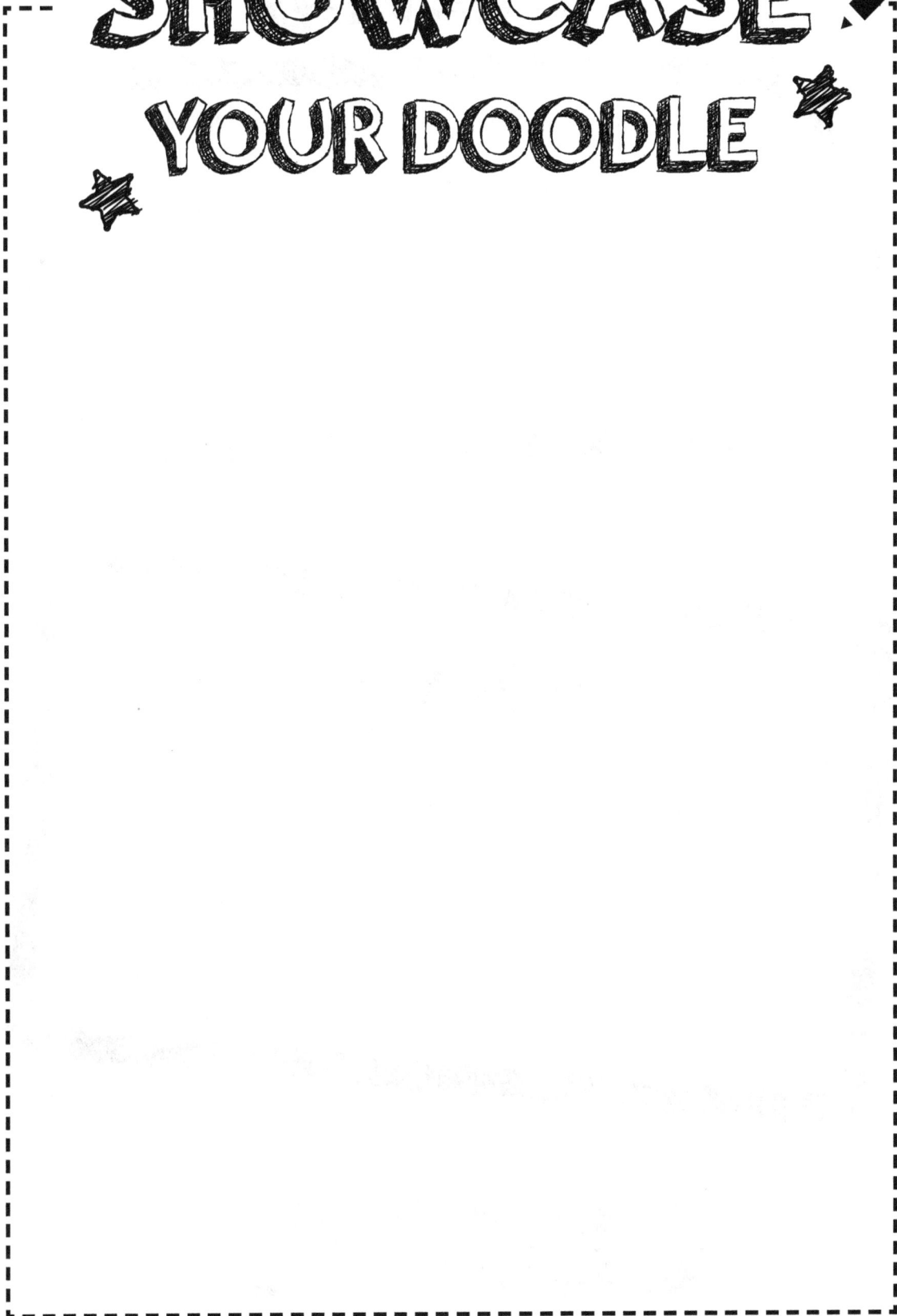

SHOWCASE
YOUR DOODLE

SKETCH

DRAW

CREATE

Doodle
and Beyond

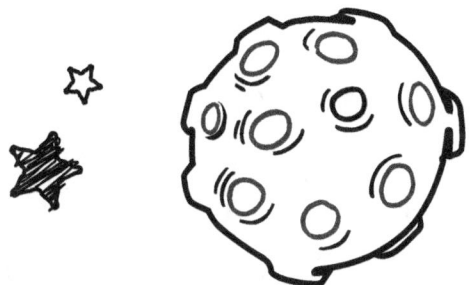

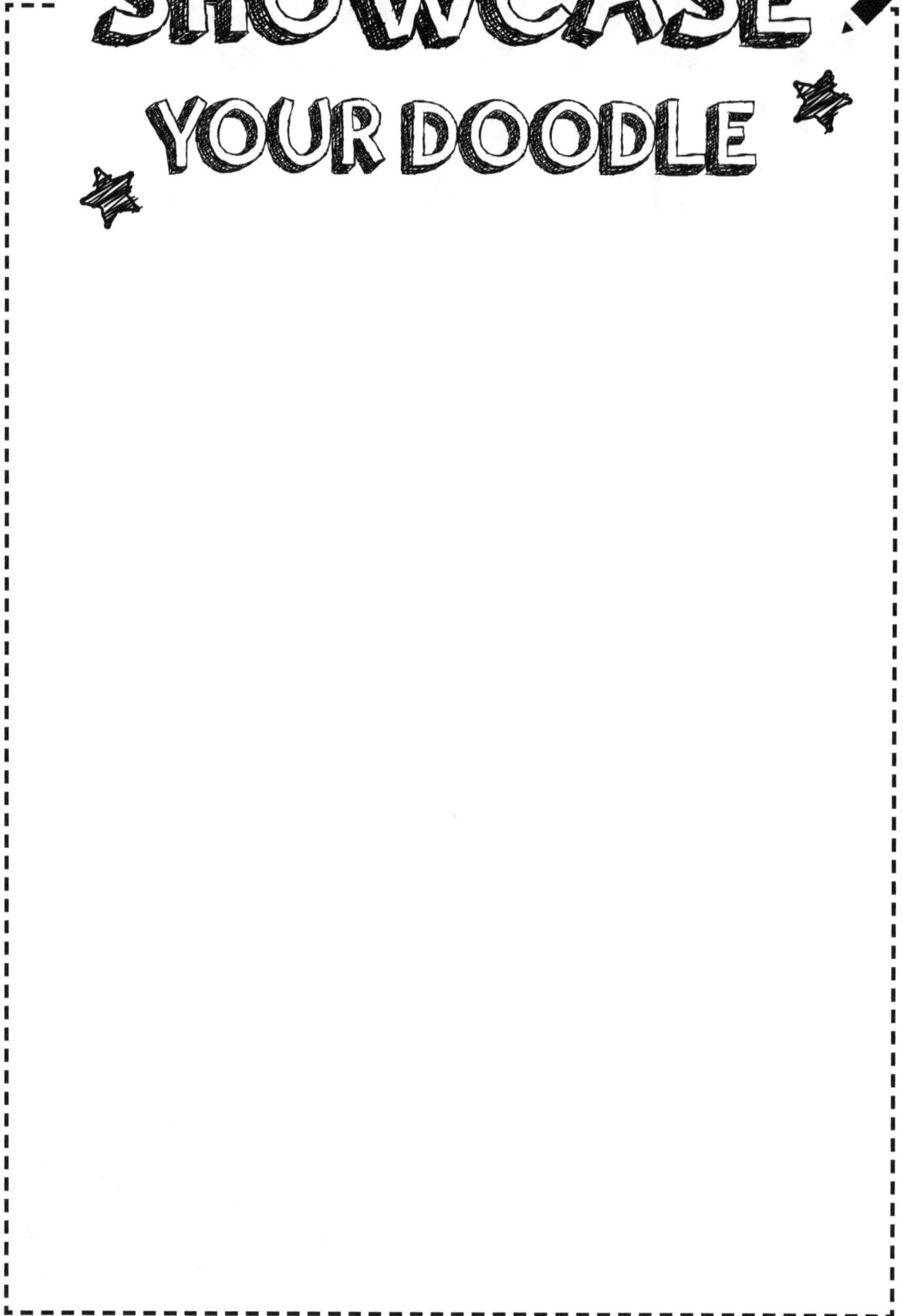

SHOWCASE
YOUR DOODLE

SKETCH

DRAW

CREATE

Doodle
and Beyond

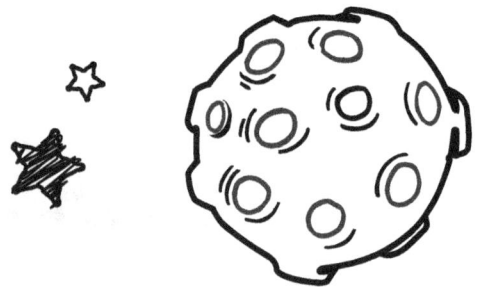

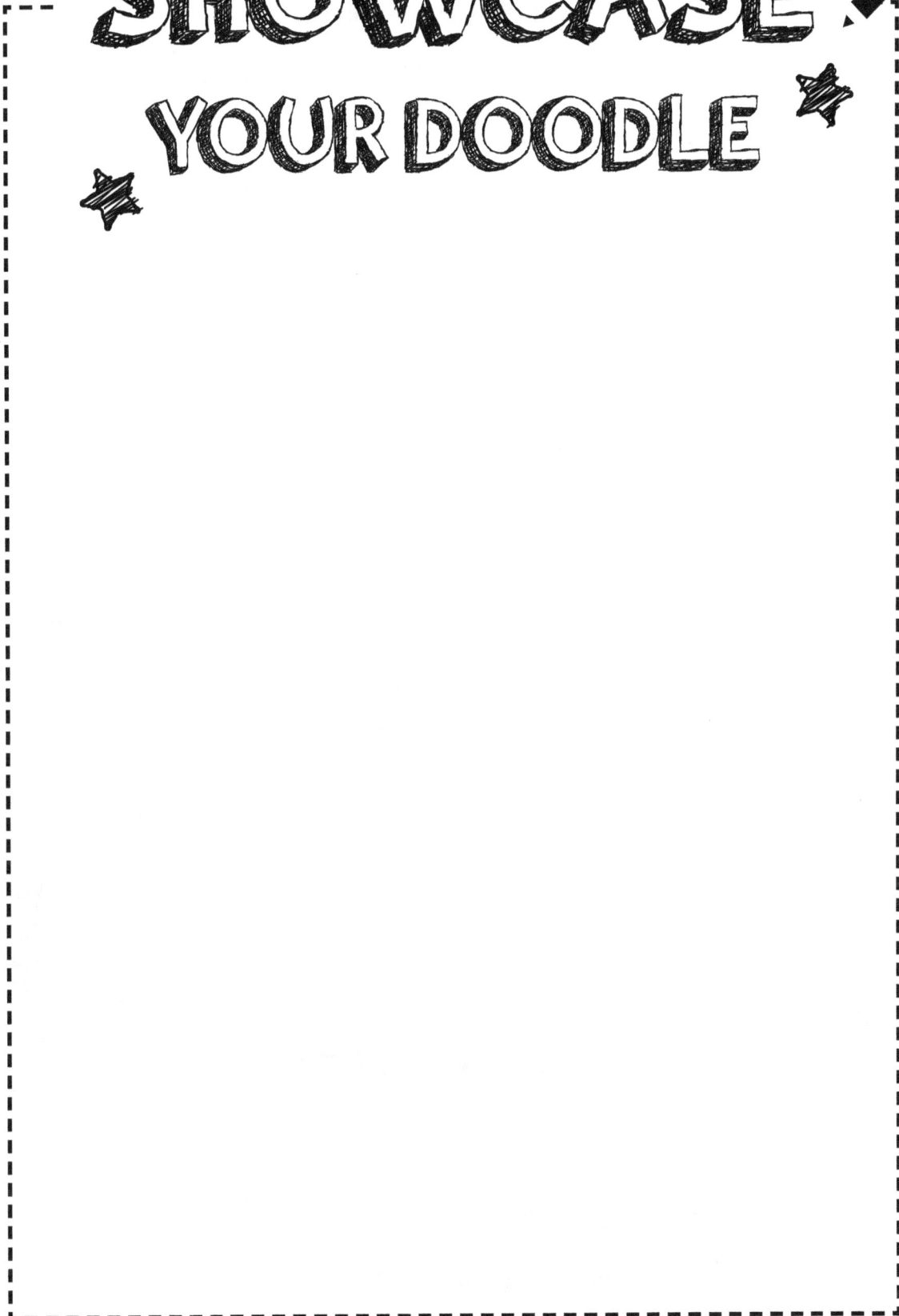

SHOWCASE
YOUR DOODLE

SKETCH

DRAW

CREATE

Doodle
and Beyond

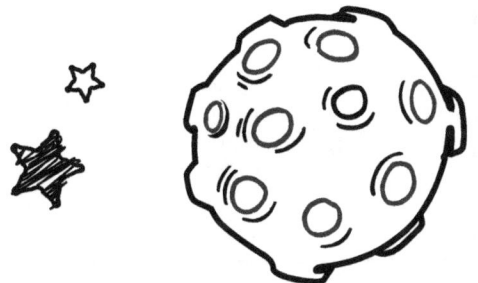

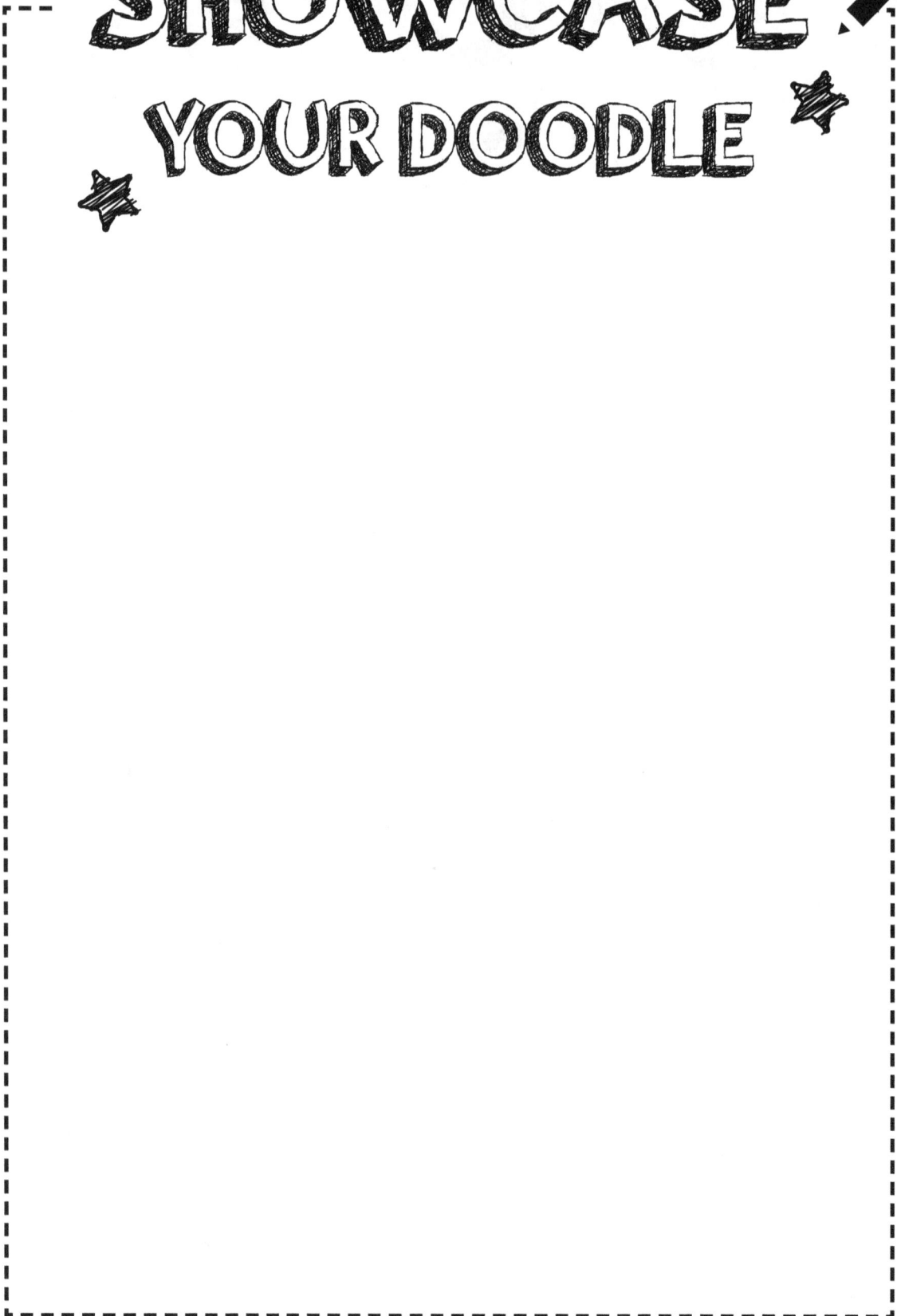

SHOWCASE
YOUR DOODLE

SKETCH

DRAW

CREATE

Doodle
and Beyond

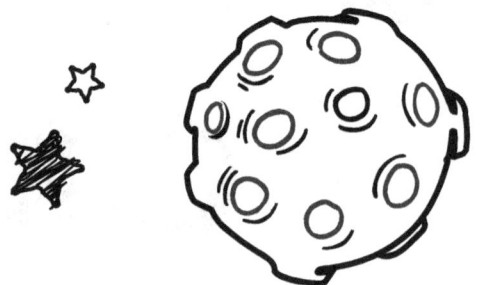

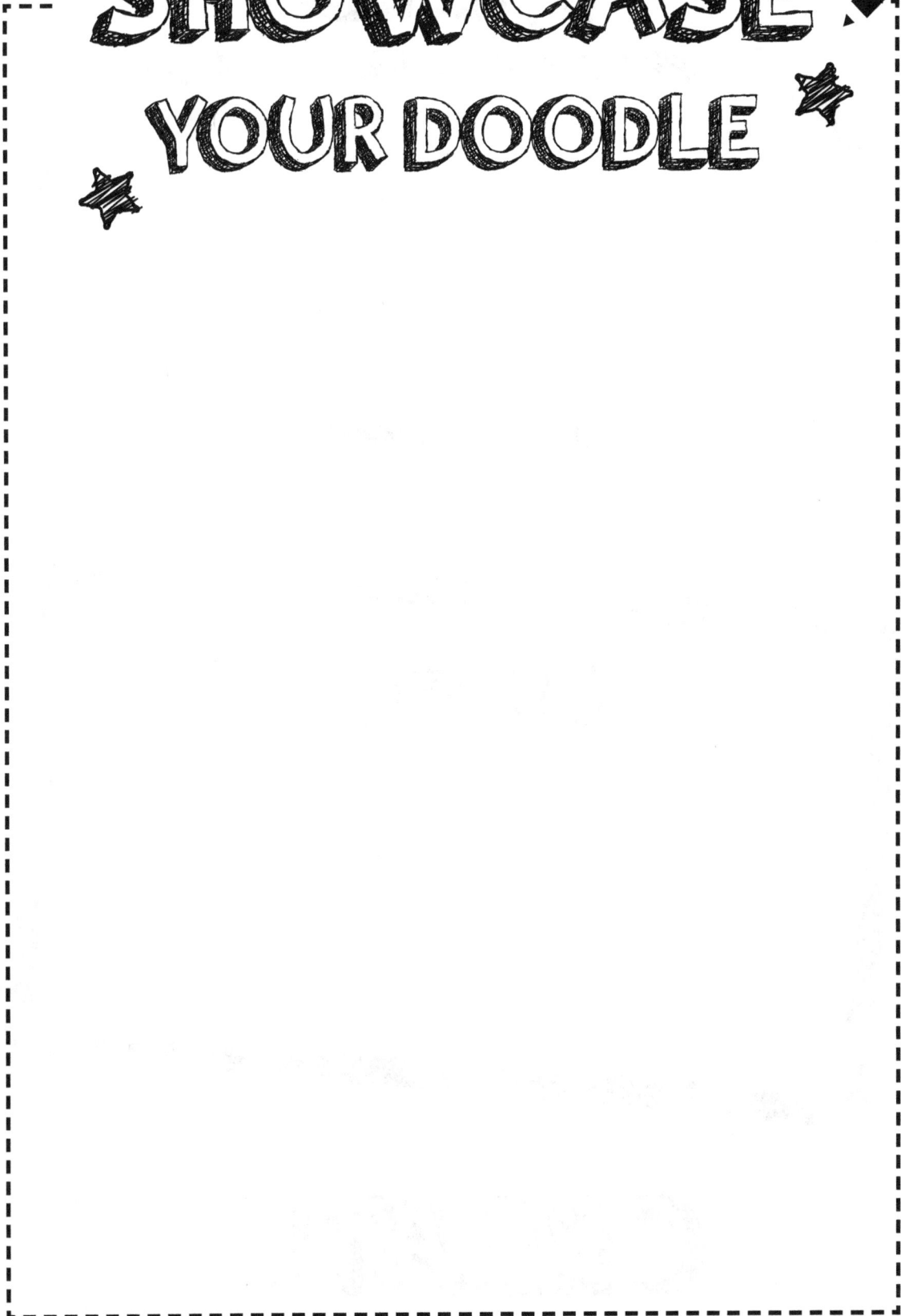

SHOWCASE
YOUR DOODLE

SKETCH

DRAW

CREATE

Doodle
and Beyond

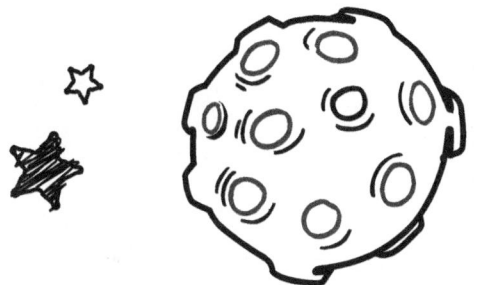

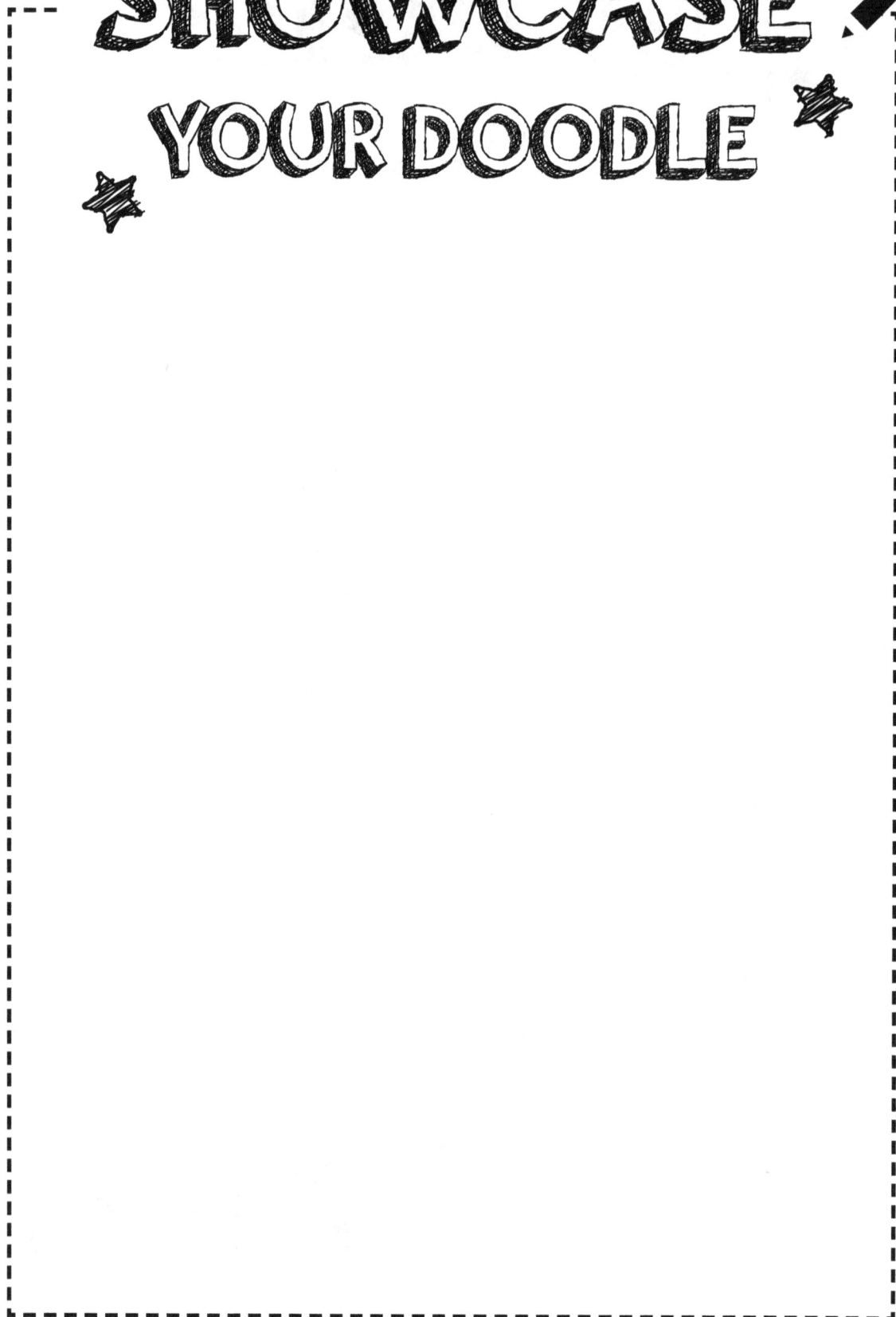

SHOWCASE
YOUR DOODLE

SKETCH

DRAW

CREATE

Doodle
and Beyond

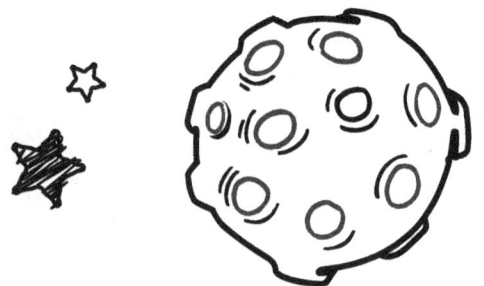

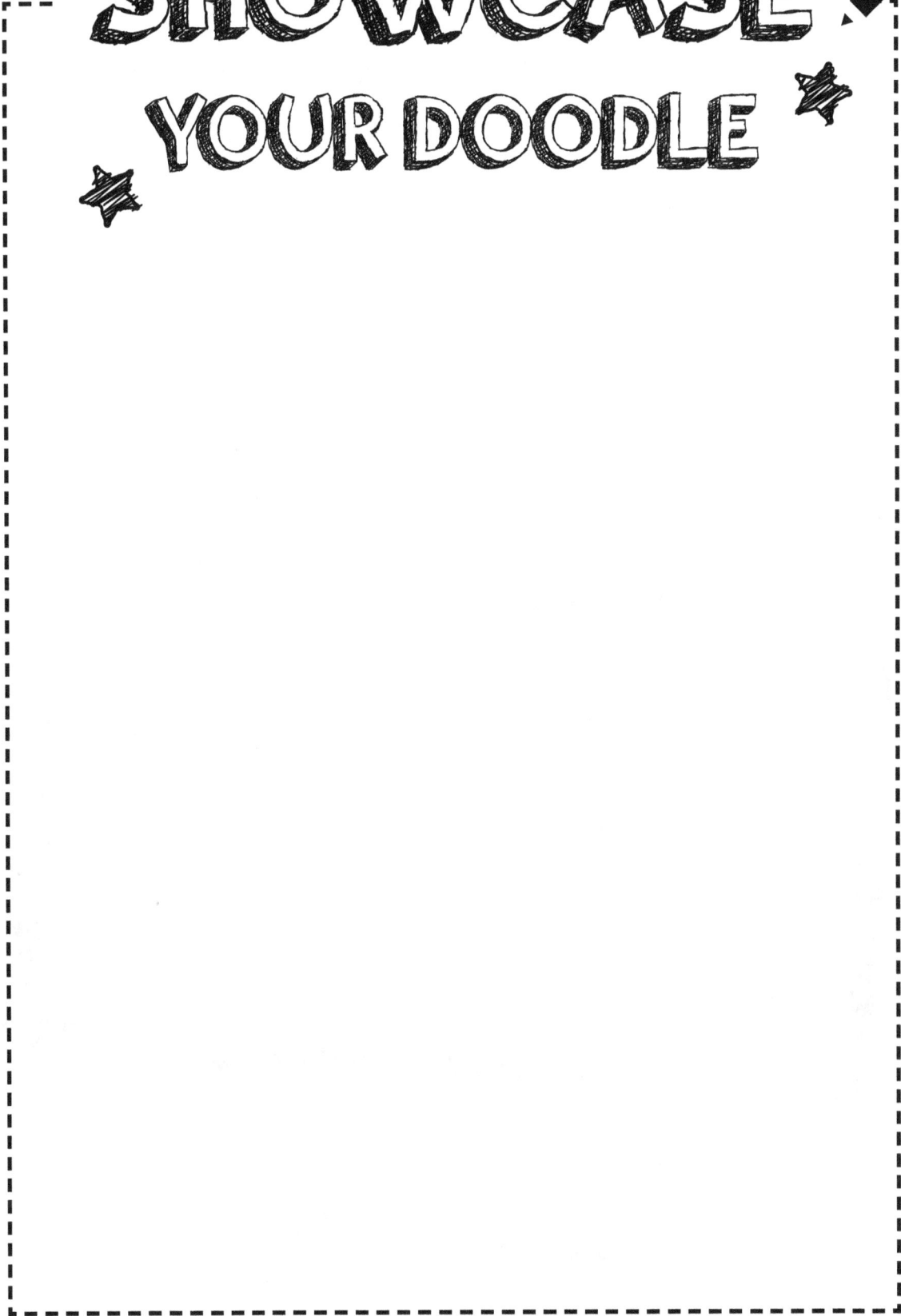

SHOWCASE
YOUR DOODLE

SKETCH

DRAW

CREATE

Doodle
and Beyond

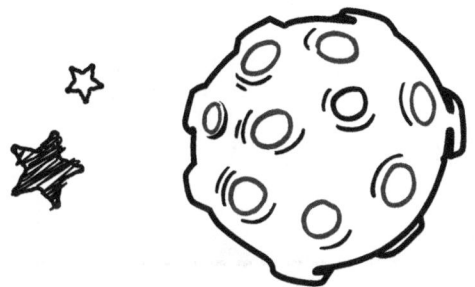

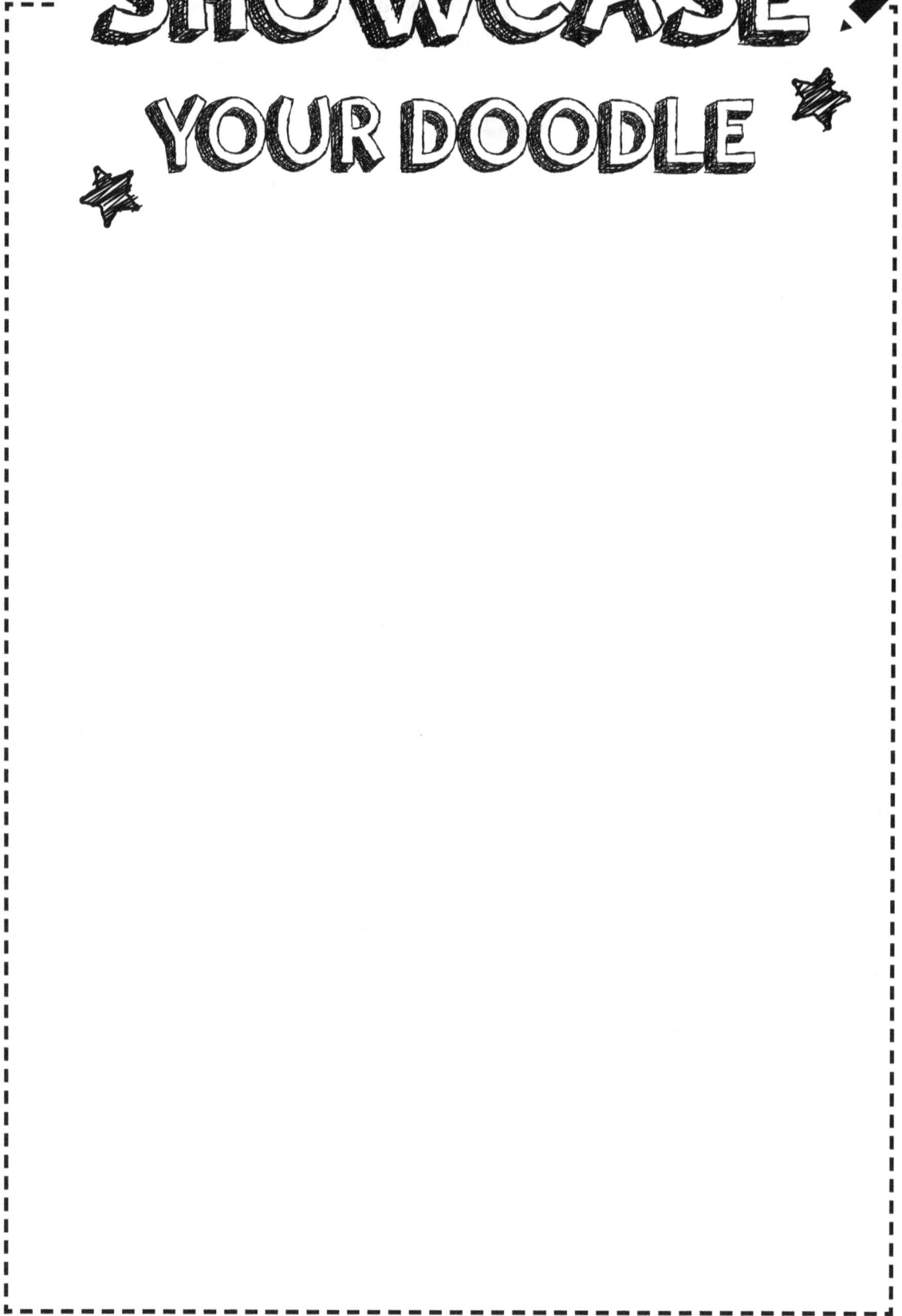

SHOWCASE
YOUR DOODLE

SKETCH

DRAW

CREATE

Doodle
and Beyond

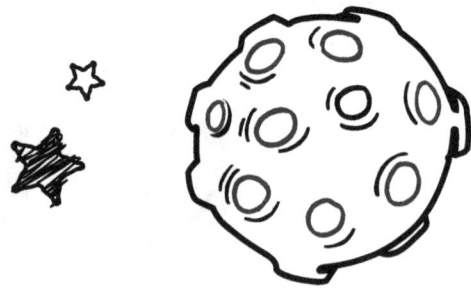

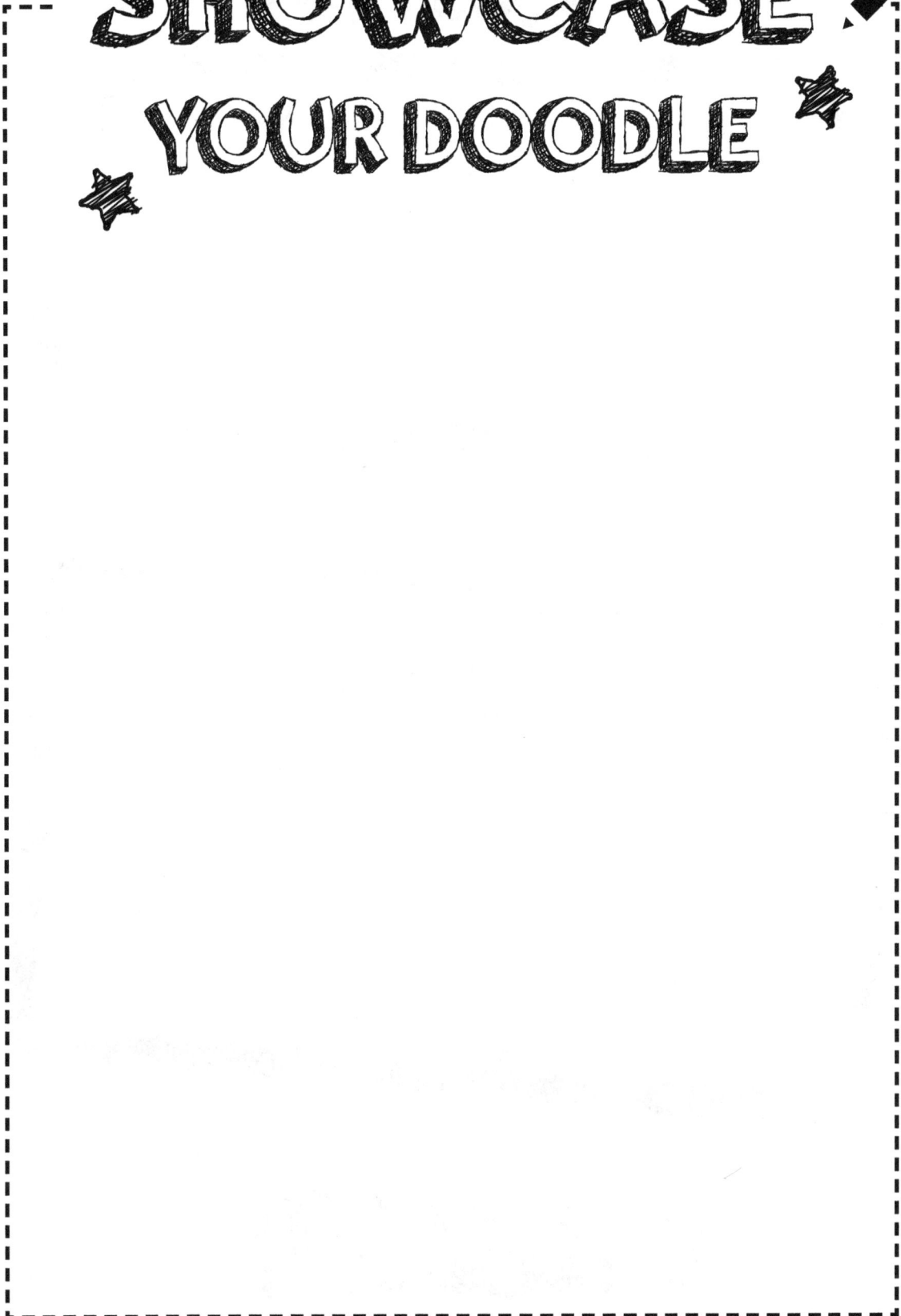

SHOWCASE
YOUR DOODLE

SKETCH

DRAW

CREATE

Doodle
and Beyond

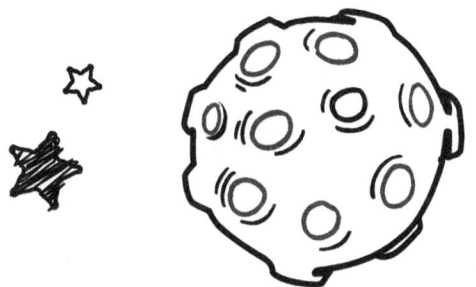

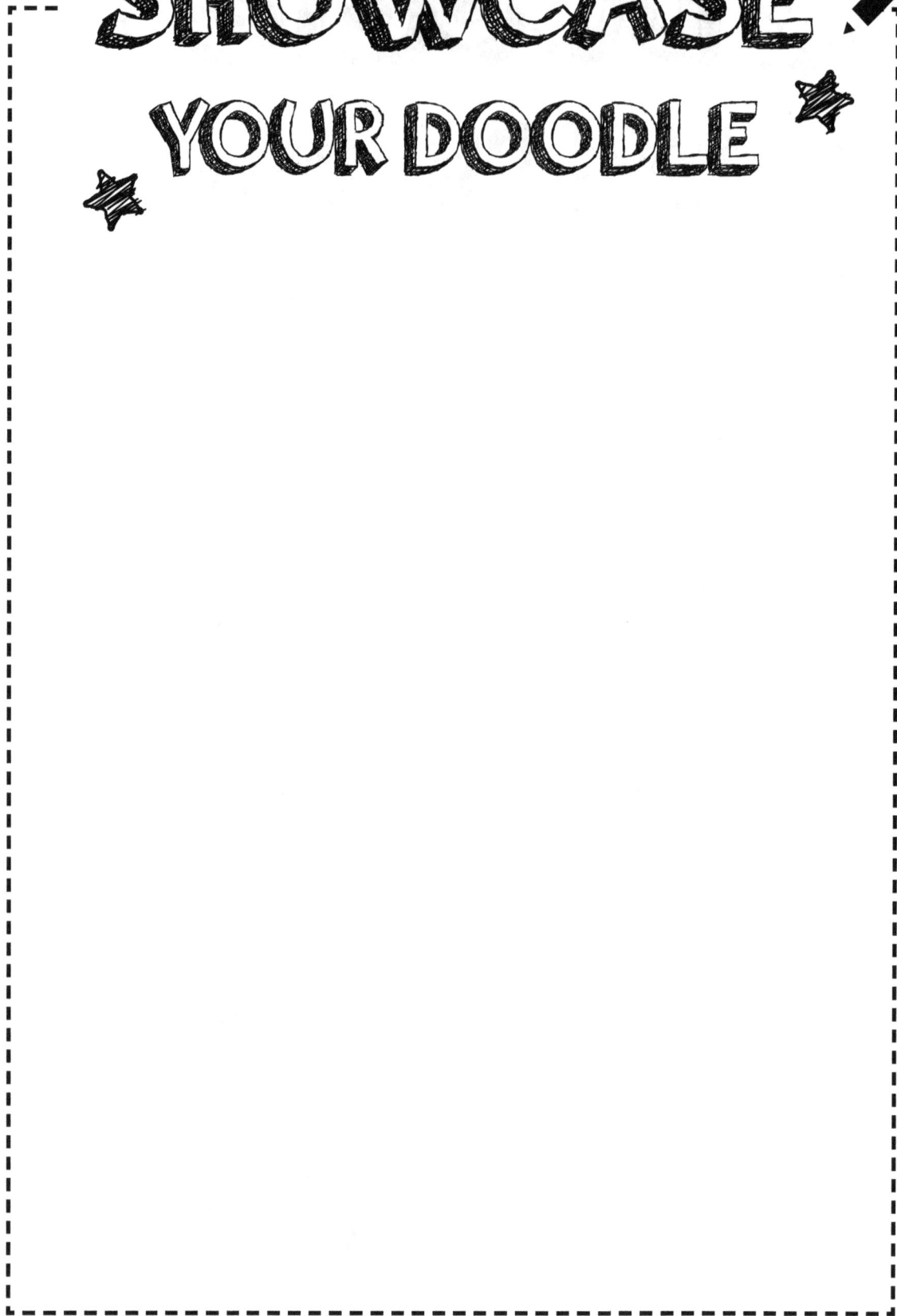

SHOWCASE
YOUR DOODLE

SKETCH

DRAW

CREATE

Doodle
and Beyond

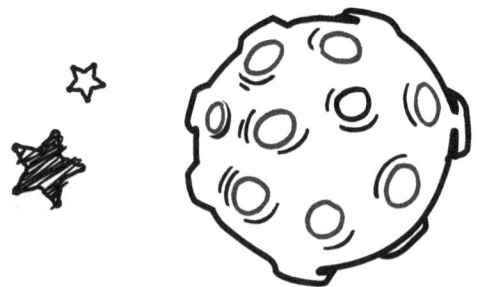

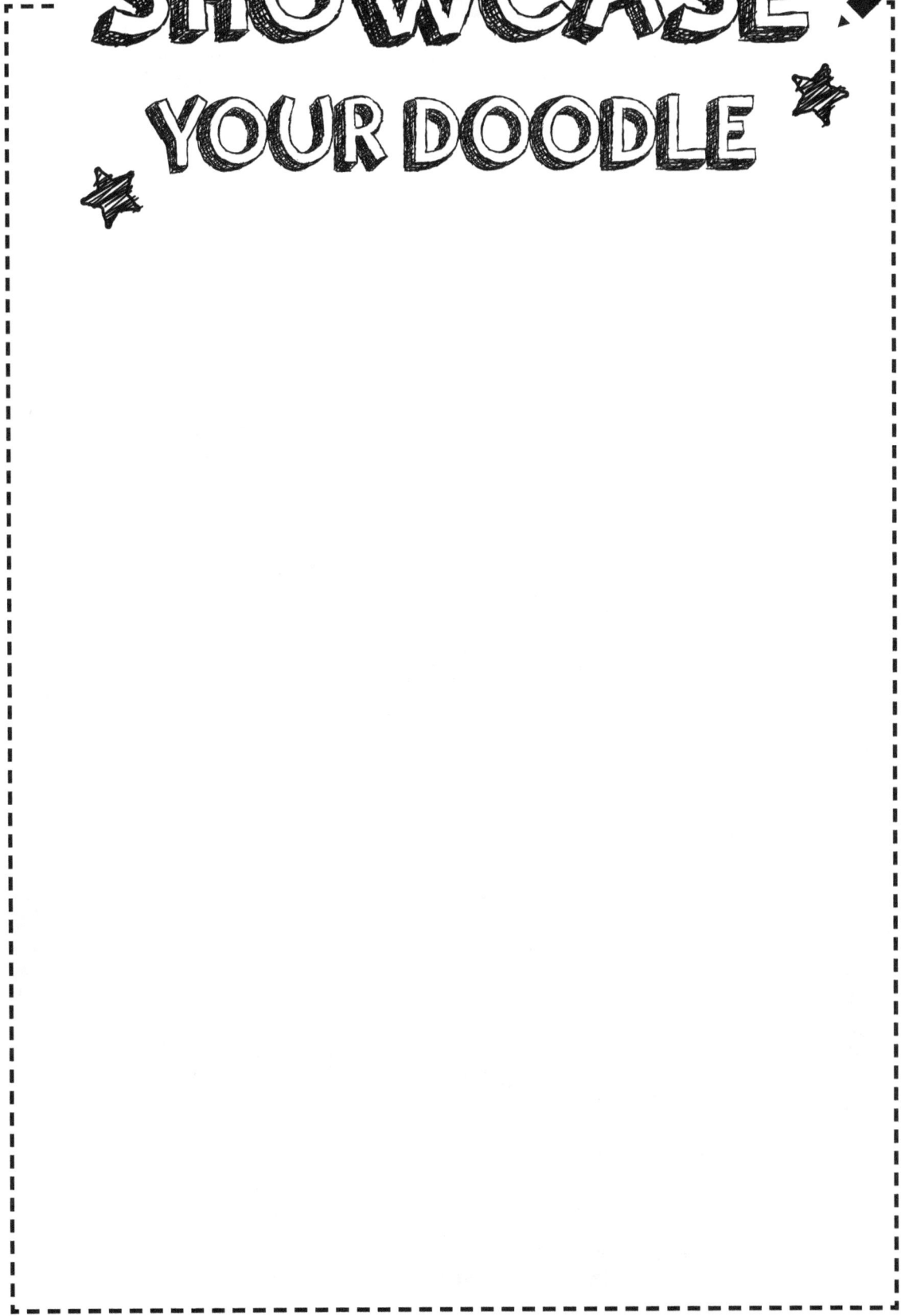

SHOWCASE
YOUR DOODLE

SKETCH

DRAW

CREATE

Doodle
and Beyond

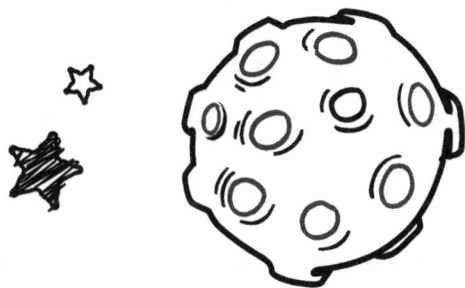

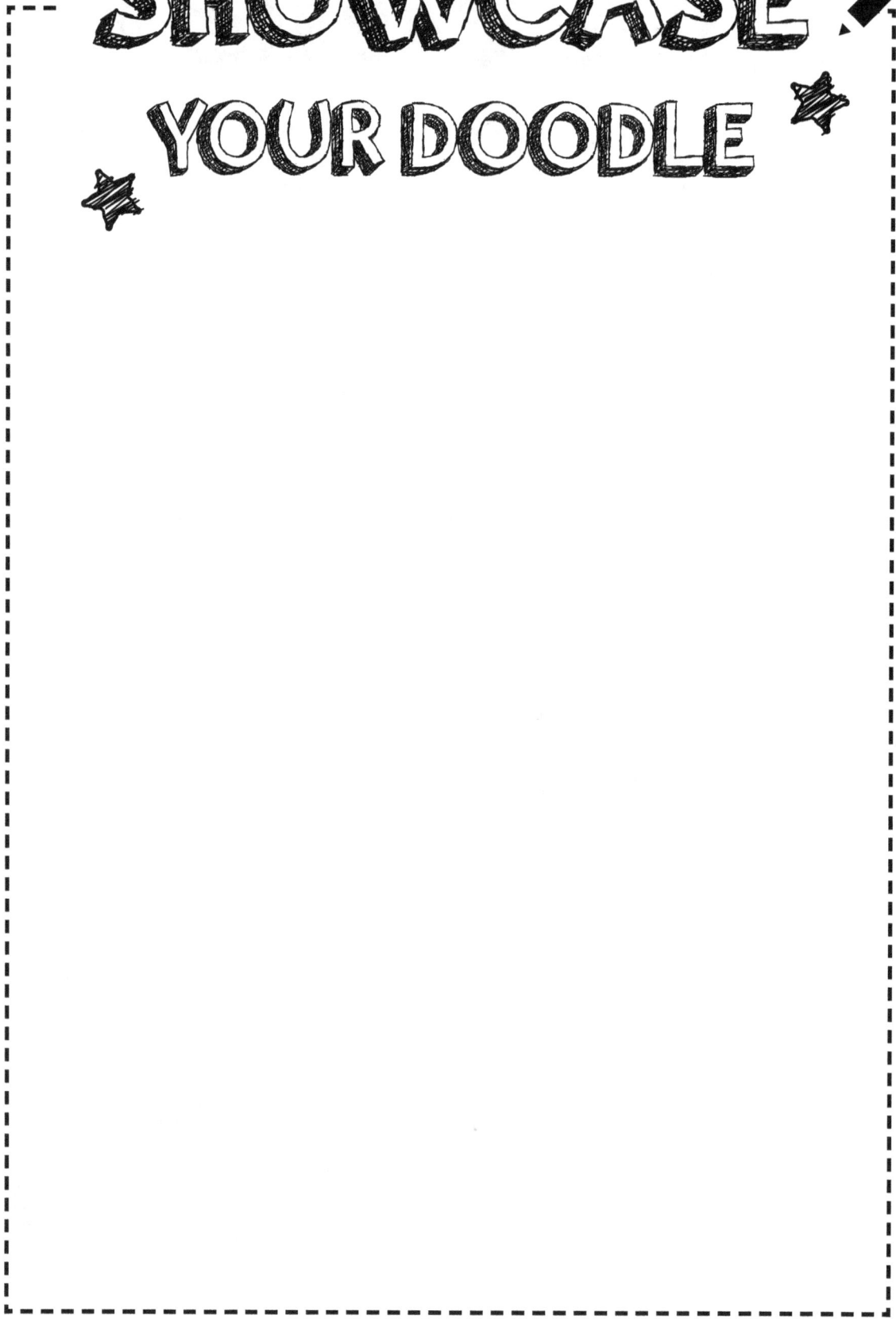

SHOWCASE
YOUR DOODLE

SKETCH

DRAW

CREATE

Doodle
and Beyond

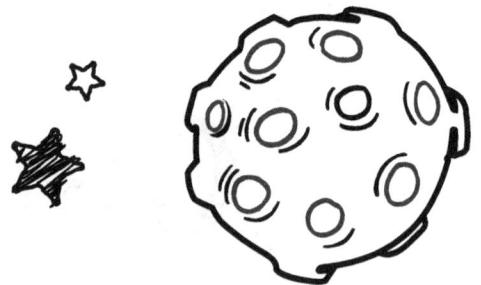

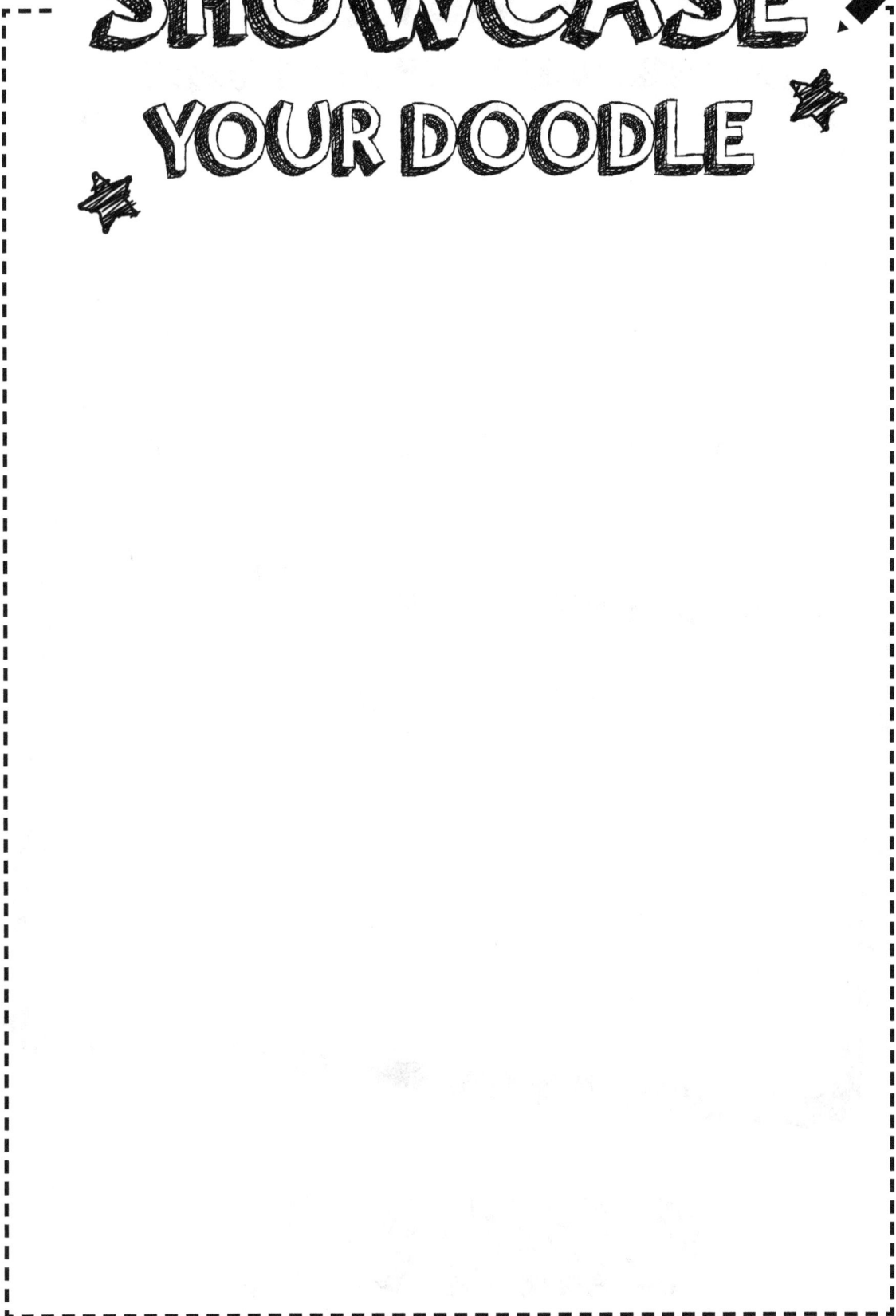

SHOWCASE
YOUR DOODLE

SKETCH

DRAW

CREATE

Doodle and Beyond

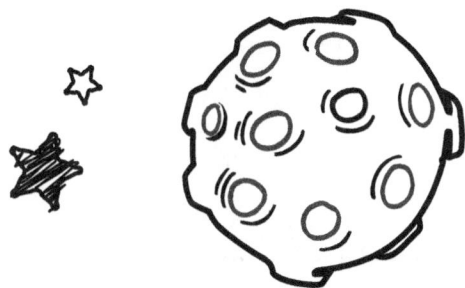

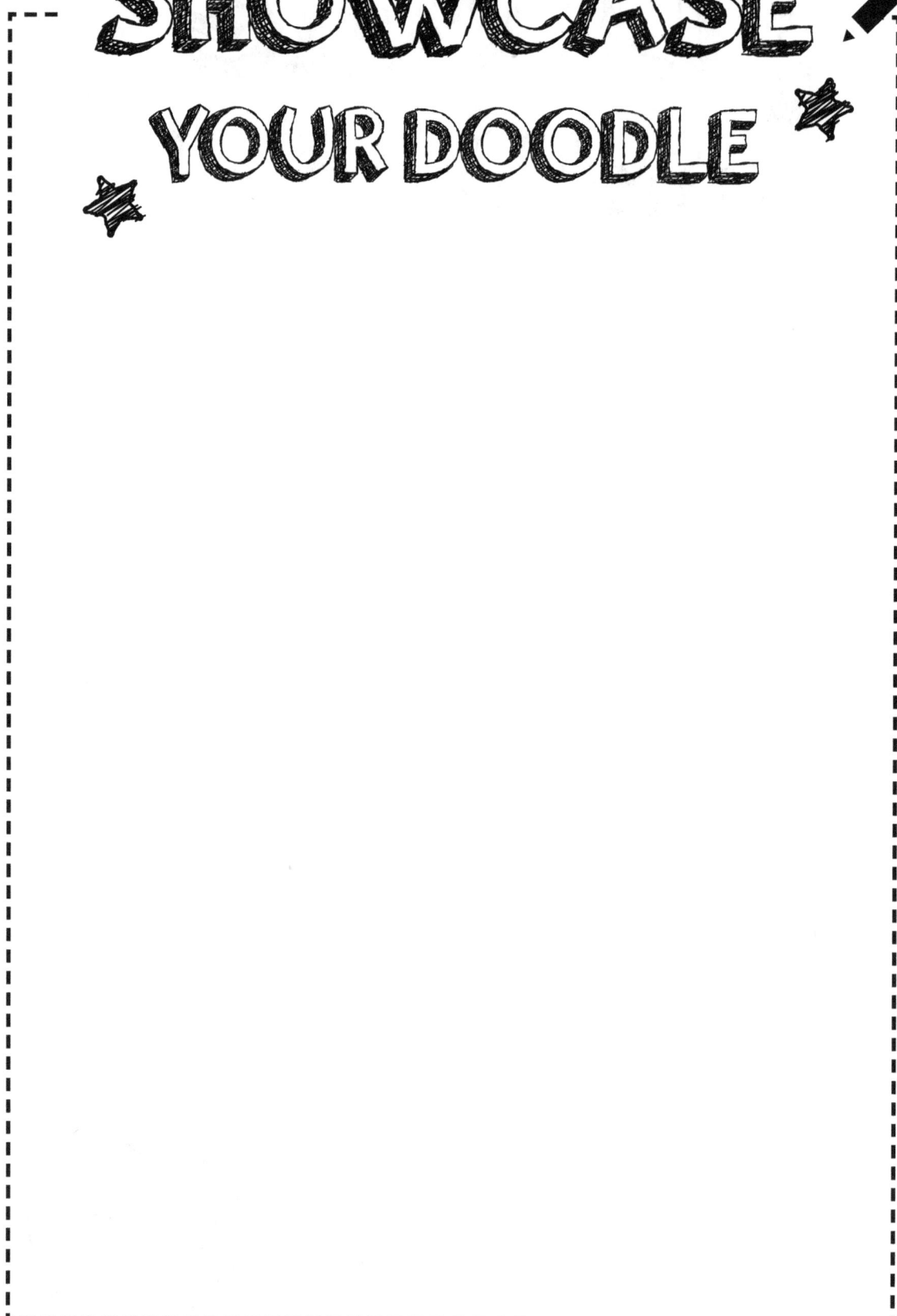

SHOWCASE
YOUR DOODLE

SKETCH

DRAW

CREATE

Doodle
and Beyond

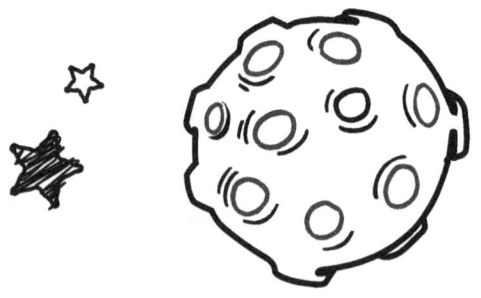

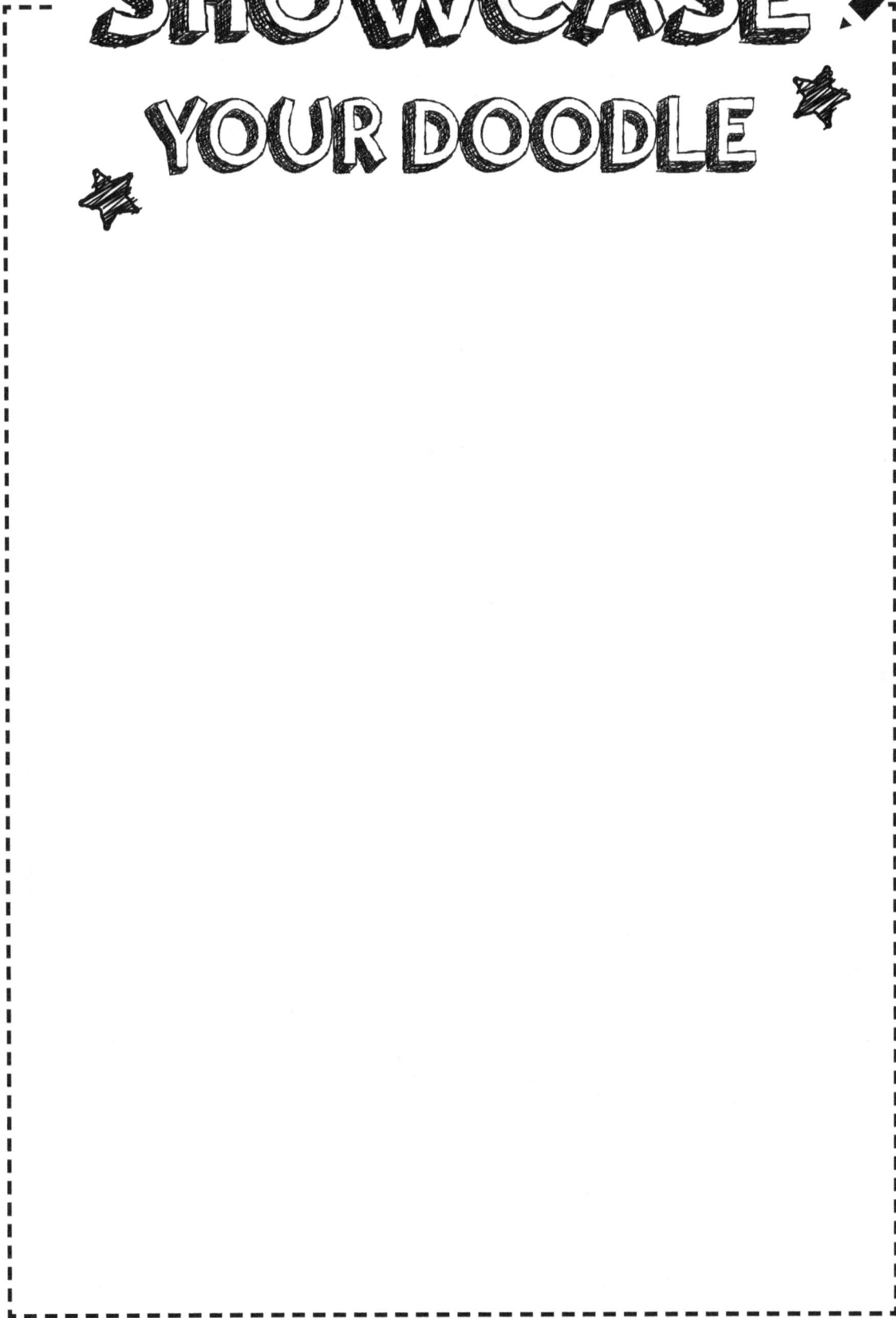

SHOWCASE
YOUR DOODLE

SKETCH

DRAW

CREATE

Doodle
and Beyond

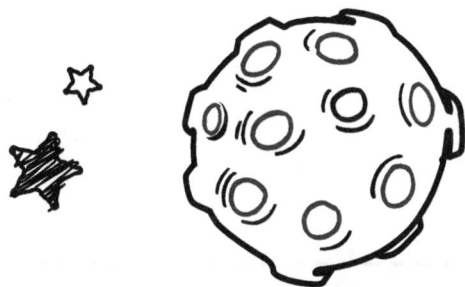

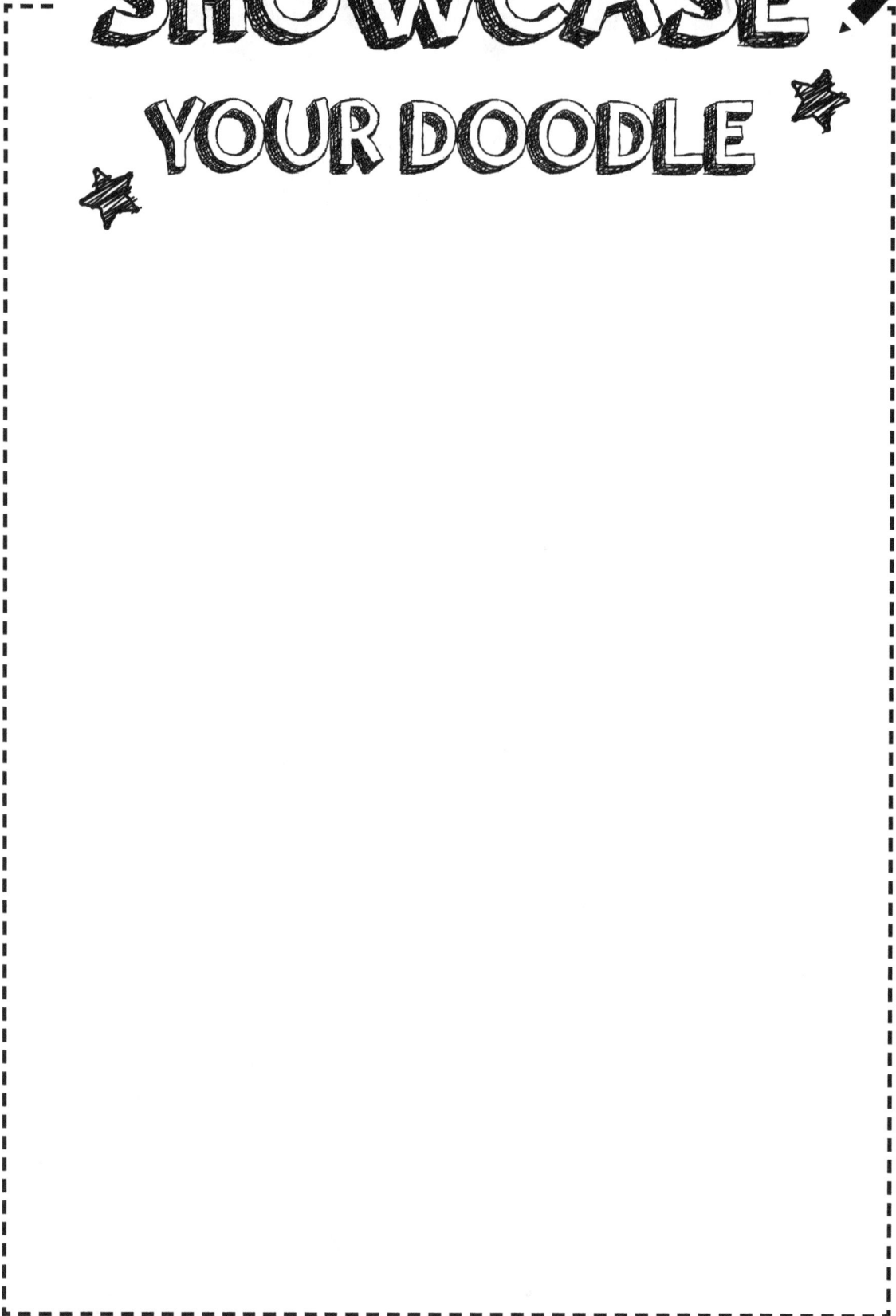

SHOWCASE
YOUR DOODLE

SKETCH

DRAW

CREATE

Doodle
and Beyond

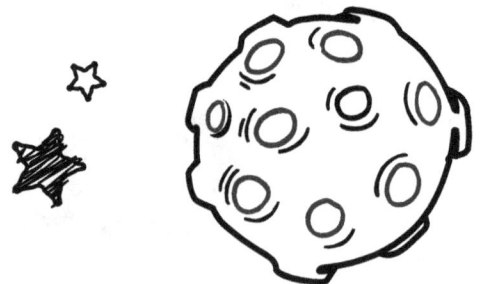

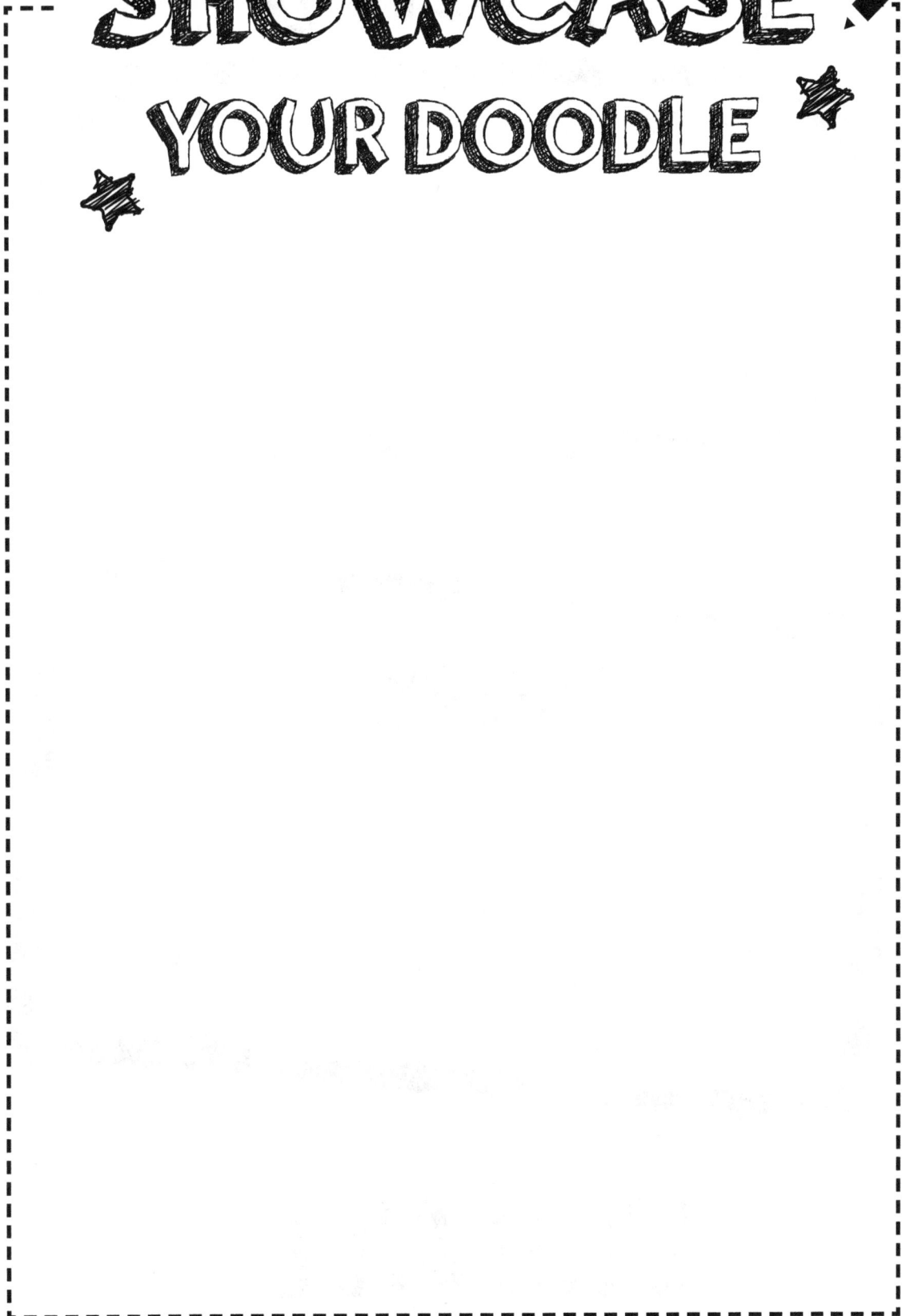

SHOWCASE
YOUR DOODLE

SKETCH

DRAW

CREATE

Doodle
and Beyond

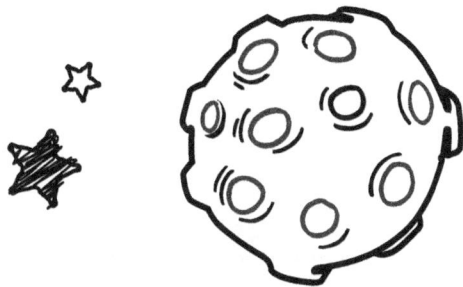

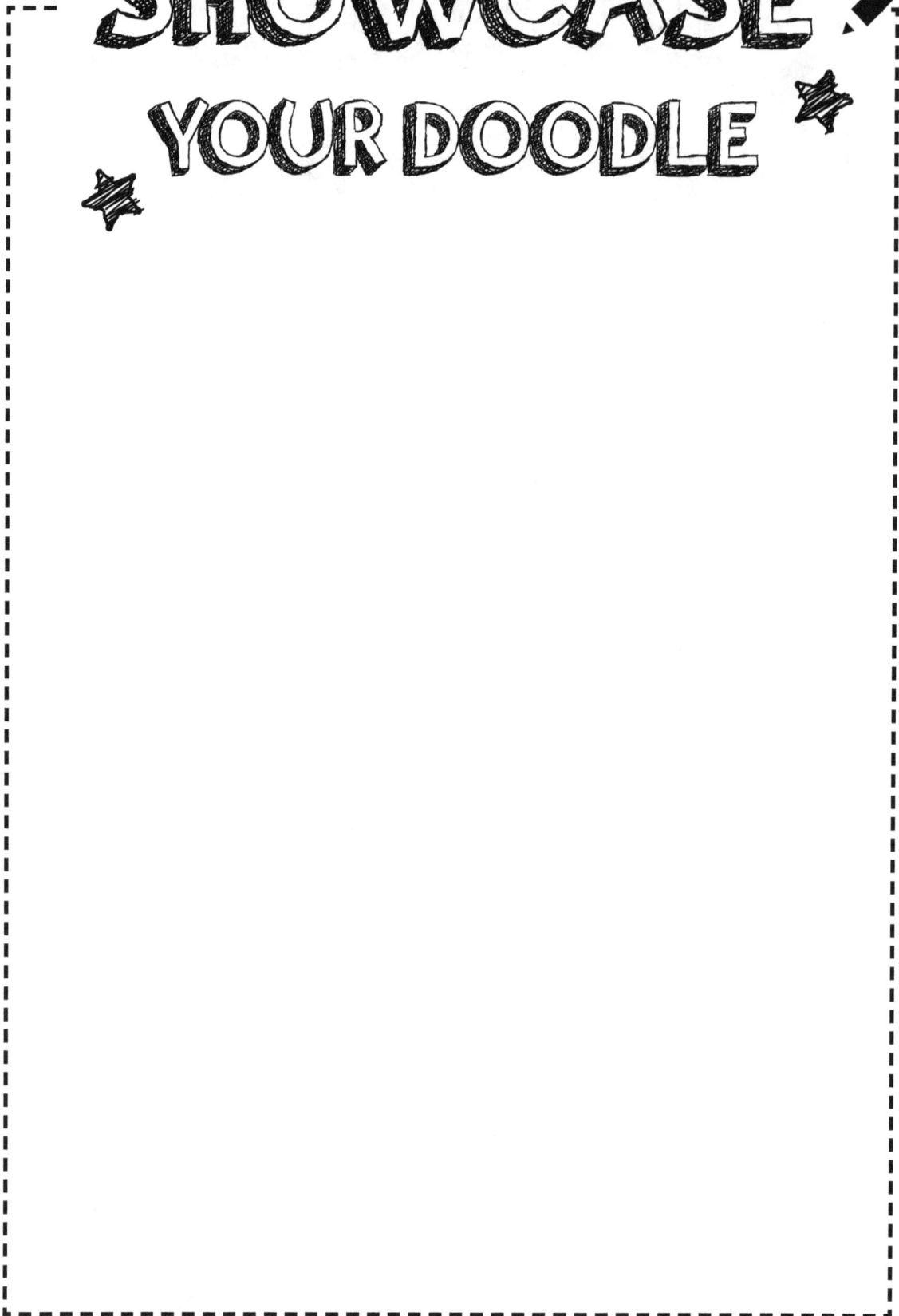

SHOWCASE
YOUR DOODLE

SKETCH

DRAW

CREATE

Doodle
and Beyond

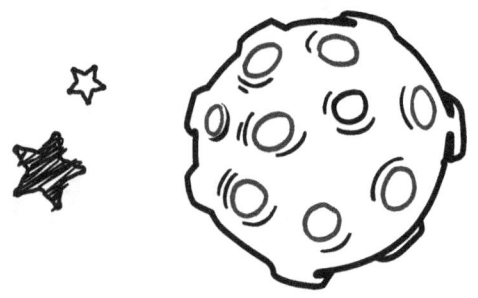

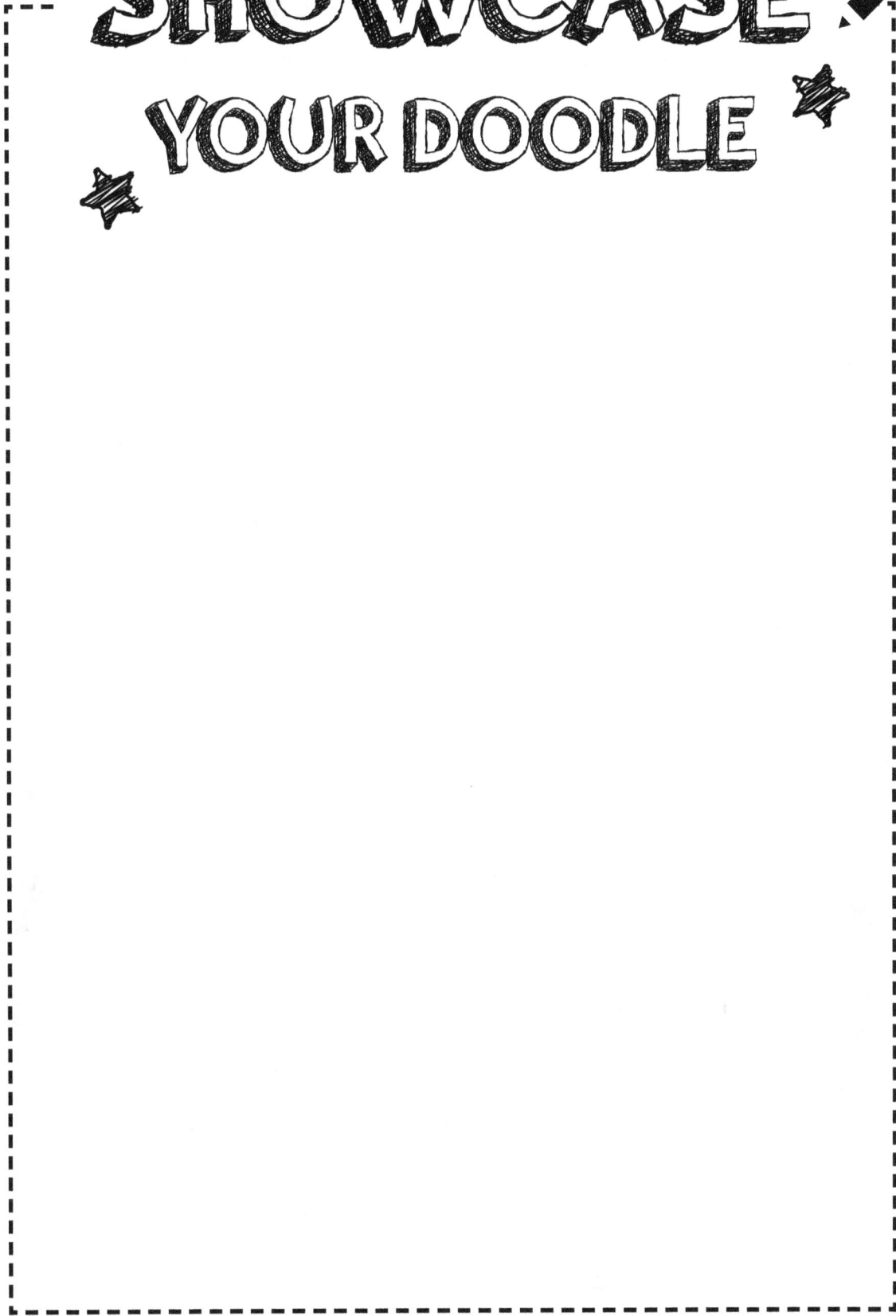

SHOWCASE
YOUR DOODLE

SKETCH

DRAW

CREATE

Doodle
and Beyond

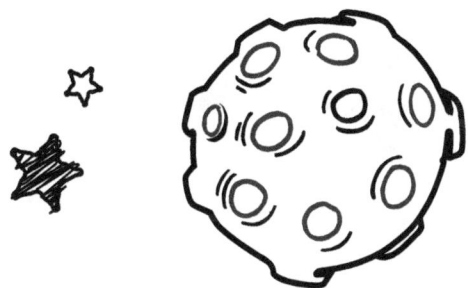

www.ingramcontent.com/pod-product-compliance
Lightning Source LLC
Chambersburg PA
CBHW081337090426
42737CB00017B/3179